THE COM

USER G

CW01498453

FOR

iPHONE 16 SERIES

Step by Step Instructions,
Hidden Features, iOS 17,
Security, Advanced Tips and
Tricks, Secret Siri Commands,
FAQs and More

ALEX HARPER

Disclaimer

This book is an independent guide and is not officially endorsed or authorized by Apple Inc. The information contained herein is based on the author's research and understanding of the iPhone 16 series and iOS 17 features at the time of publication. While every effort has been made to ensure the accuracy of the content, the author and publisher cannot be held liable for any errors or omissions. For official information and updates, please refer to Apple Inc.'s official documentation and support resources.

TABLE OF CONTENTS

INTRODUCTION

*****

The release of the iPhone 16 series marks a significant leap forward in mobile technology, setting a new standard for smartphones across the globe. With each iteration, Apple continues to push the envelope in design, functionality, and user experience, and the iPhone 16 is no exception. The iPhone 16, iPhone 16 Pro and iPhone 16 Pro Max have brought innovations that promise to redefine how users interact with their devices daily. Whether you're a long-time iPhone enthusiast or new to the Apple ecosystem, the iPhone 16 series has something to offer everyone.

Overview of the iPhone 16 Series

The iPhone 16 series is more than just another smartphone lineup; it combines cutting-edge technology, sleek design, and software enhancements that cater to the modern user's needs. Apple's approach with the iPhone 16 series has been focused on elevating the user experience through meaningful improvements, not just surface-level changes. While the outward appearance may resemble the iPhone 15, a closer look reveals a host of advancements that make the iPhone 16 series an undeniable upgrade.

Design and Display

At first glance, the iPhone 16, iPhone 16 Pro, and iPhone 16 Pro Max maintains the signature sleek, minimalistic design Apple is known for. However, subtle refinements have been made to improve the overall feel and durability of the device. The new aerospace-grade aluminum and stainless steel frame used in the Pro models offer greater durability without adding extra weight and the glass back and ceramic shield on the front remain but have been improved for even better drop protection.

The display is one of the standout features of the iPhone 16 series. The Super Retina XDR display has been further enhanced to offer a sharper, brighter, and more color-accurate visual experience. The iPhone 16 models now feature ProMotion technology, which allows for an adaptive refresh rate of up to 120Hz. This means smoother scrolling, quicker response times, and a more immersive experience whether you're playing games, watching videos, or just browsing. The Pro Max model, with its larger 6.9-inch display, offers an unparalleled viewing experience that will make even the most demanding users take notice.

Performance and Processor

Under the hood, the iPhone 16 series is powered by the new A18 Bionic chip, which is faster, more efficient, and designed to handle intensive tasks without breaking a sweat. This chip is built on a 3-nanometer architecture, making it the most advanced mobile processor Apple has ever created. Whether you're multitasking across several apps, editing 4K video on the go, or engaging in high-end mobile gaming, the A18 Bionic chip ensures that everything runs smoothly without lag or stutter.

The Neural Engine within the A18 has also been upgraded to handle AI-based tasks with greater efficiency. From real-time translation to advanced image processing, the Neural Engine is at the heart of the iPhone 16's capabilities. Machine learning tasks are now faster and more responsive, enhancing everything from Face ID recognition to app predictions.

Camera System

Apple has made significant strides in improving the camera system with each new iPhone model, and the iPhone 16 series takes it to the next level. The standard iPhone 16 features a dual-camera system, while the iPhone 16 Pro and Pro Max models boast a more sophisticated triple-camera setup. The Pro models include a 48MP main sensor, which provides stunning detail and clarity in photos, particularly in low-light conditions.

A major new feature in the Pro and Pro Max models is the addition of a periscope-style telephoto lens, allowing for up to 10x optical zoom. This feature will revolutionize mobile photography, enabling users to capture distant subjects with unprecedented detail. The improved night mode, enhanced computational photography, and better image stabilization are also key highlights, making the iPhone 16 camera system ideal for both casual users and professionals alike.

Battery Life and Charging

Apple has continued to optimize battery life with the iPhone 16 series, ensuring that users can go about their day without worrying about frequent charging. The efficiency of the A18 Bionic chip, combined with a larger battery, means that the iPhone 16 can last significantly longer on a single charge compared to its predecessors. Whether you're using the iPhone for work, entertainment, or navigation, you can expect several hours of extra usage with the iPhone 16 models.

Fast charging has also been improved, with the Pro models supporting up to 50% charge in just 20 minutes. Apple's MagSafe technology remains a convenient option for wireless charging, and improvements in heat management mean that the iPhone 16 can charge faster and more safely than previous models.

Why Choose the iPhone 16?

With so many smartphones on the market, users are often left wondering why they should upgrade or consider the latest model. The iPhone 16 series addresses this question by offering several compelling reasons to make the switch, even for those who own the iPhone 15.

Enhanced Performance for Power Users

For users who demand the best in performance, the iPhone 16 series is a no-brainer. The A18 Bionic chip is not just an incremental upgrade—it's a game-changer. Its speed, efficiency, and ability to handle intensive tasks put it miles ahead of competitors. Either you're a content creator, a professional photographer, or someone who simply wants the best possible experience, the iPhone 16 delivers on all fronts.

Unmatched Display Quality

The ProMotion display on the iPhone 16, with its 120Hz adaptive refresh rate, offers a viewing experience like no other. Whether you're binge-watching your favorite series or gaming, the fluidity of motion, combined with the vividness of colors, creates an experience that's hard to replicate. If you're someone who uses their phone for media consumption or creative work, the iPhone 16 Pro and Pro Max are the best options available.

Revolutionary Camera Capabilities

If you're passionate about photography or videography, the iPhone 16 series will elevate your content. The new 48MP camera with enhanced low-light performance and the periscope lens on the Pro models make it possible to capture professional-quality images right from your pocket. The improvements to computational photography, including smarter HDR and enhanced night mode, mean that your photos will look incredible regardless of the lighting conditions. The 10x optical zoom is also a game-changer for capturing subjects at a distance, making the Pro Max model the ideal choice for photography enthusiasts.

Future-Proofing Your Investment

One of the main reasons to choose the iPhone 16 is the assurance that you're getting a future-proof device. With regular iOS updates, superior build quality, and access to Apple's ecosystem, the iPhone 16 series is designed to remain relevant and functional for years to come. Apple's commitment to software support ensures that even as new features and apps are introduced, your iPhone 16 will be able to handle them without issues.

Security and Privacy Features

In a world where data privacy is of paramount importance, the iPhone 16 series offers industry-leading security features. From Face ID, which is faster and more accurate than ever, to Apple's new privacy-focused tools like Mail Privacy Protection, App Tracking Transparency, and Private Relay, users can feel confident that their data is safe and secure. If privacy is a key concern for you, the iPhone 16's comprehensive suite of security features provides peace of mind in a digital age.

Integration with Apple's Ecosystem

One of the best reasons to consider upgrading to the iPhone 16 is its seamless integration with Apple's broader ecosystem. Whether you use an Apple Watch, iPad, MacBook, or AirPods, the iPhone 16 acts as the central hub for your digital life. Handoff, AirDrop, Continuity Camera, and other Apple-exclusive features work even better on the iPhone 16, making it the ideal companion for users already invested in the Apple ecosystem.

Guide Purpose

The purpose of this guide is to provide users with a comprehensive understanding of the iPhone 16, iPhone 16 Pro, and iPhone 16 Pro Max, empowering them to maximize the use of their devices. Whether you're upgrading from an older model or transitioning from a different operating system, this guide will walk you through every aspect of the iPhone 16 series, from setup and customization to advanced features and troubleshooting.

Who Is This Guide For?

This guide is designed for everyone—from first-time iPhone users to experienced tech enthusiasts. If you're a casual user looking to get the most out of your phone, we'll cover the basics of setup, customization, and everyday usage. If you're a power user, this guide will dive deep into the more advanced features, such as performance optimization, professional photography tips, and the intricacies of iOS 17.

What Can You Expect?

In this guide, you can expect easy-to-follow instructions, expert tips, and visual aids that will make navigating the iPhone 16 a seamless experience. **We will cover topics like:**

- First-time setup and transferring data from your old phone.
- Customizing the Home Screen, widgets, and notifications to match your lifestyle.
- Exploring iOS 17 features and Apple's ecosystem services like iCloud, Apple Pay, and Apple Music.
- Mastering the iPhone 16's camera and editing tools for professional quality content.
- Troubleshooting common problems and learning how to optimize battery life.

Maximizing Your iPhone Experience

Our goal is to ensure that you're not just using your iPhone 16 but truly leveraging its full potential. This guide will provide a roadmap to mastering your device, whether it's for work, entertainment, or creative expression. Each chapter will build upon the previous one, ensuring you gain confidence with every step.

This guide aims to be a complete reference for all iPhone 16 users, ensuring that you'll never feel lost, whether you're exploring new features, customizing your phone, or troubleshooting an issue. It's designed to be the one resource you'll turn to repeatedly throughout your iPhone 16 journey.

CHAPTER 1

UNBOXING AND FIRST-TIME SETUP

*****

Unboxing a new iPhone is always a moment of excitement, as it marks the beginning of a fresh experience with Apple's latest innovations. With the iPhone 16, iPhone 16 Pro, and iPhone 16 Pro Max, Apple has continued its tradition of sleek, minimal packaging, while making sure that everything you need to get started is included in the box. However, the setup process has evolved, offering new features and capabilities that maximize the efficiency of the device from the moment you power it on. In this chapter, we'll walk you through everything you need to know about what's in the box, how to set up your iPhone for the first time, and the important settings you should configure immediately.

What's in the Box

Apple's packaging for the iPhone 16 series is designed with simplicity in mind, but it still includes all the essentials you need to get started. As you open the box, here's what you'll find:

1. The iPhone 16, iPhone 16 Pro, or iPhone 16 Pro Max: The device itself, wrapped securely and resting on a protective layer, is the centerpiece of the package. Whether you've opted for the standard model or one of the Pro variants, you'll immediately notice the sleek design, refined edges, and premium materials used in the build.

2. USB-C to Lightning Cable: For charging and data transfer, the iPhone 16 comes with a USB-C to lightning cable. Apple has opted for this faster, more versatile cable to support quick charging and high-speed data transfer, while still maintaining compatibility with existing Lightning accessories.

3. SIM Ejector Tool: This small, pin-like tool is included to help you easily remove the SIM card tray and insert your SIM card if needed. It's a useful accessory, especially for those switching from another device or needing to install a new SIM card.

4. Documentation: Inside the box, you'll find a minimalistic set of paper documents, including quick start guide and warranty information. While Apple has moved away from including lengthy manuals, the included guide provides basic instructions to help you get started.

5. Apple Sticker: As a fun extra, Apple includes its signature logo sticker in the box. While this isn't essential to your iPhone experience, many Apple users enjoy using these stickers to personalize their belongings.

6. No Charging Brick: It's important to note that Apple no longer includes a charging brick in the box. This decision was made in line with Apple's sustainability efforts. However, if you do not already own a USB-C charging brick, you'll need to purchase one separately to charge your iPhone 16.

With the box opened and the contents laid out, it's time to dive into the first-time setup process for your iPhone 16. This is where you'll begin customizing the device to suit your preferences and needs.

Step-by-Step Setup

The first-time setup of your iPhone 16 is an intuitive process, but Apple's software ensures that it is thorough enough to ensure every feature is properly configured. Follow these steps to ensure a smooth and efficient setup:

1. Powering On Your iPhone

After unboxing your new iPhone, the first step is to power it on. To do this, press and hold the side button (located on the right side of the device) until the Apple logo appears on the screen. Once powered on, the device will guide you through the setup process with on-screen instructions.

2. Choosing Your Language and Region

Once the phone is powered on, you'll be prompted to select your preferred language. This is important because it determines the default language for the interface, including menus, apps, and system settings. After selecting your language, you'll also need to choose your region or country. This affects settings like time zones, regional formats, and content availability in the App Store.

3. Connecting to Wi-Fi

Next, your iPhone will prompt you to connect to a Wi-Fi network. This is a critical step because it allows the device to communicate with Apple's servers, download updates, and sync your data. Choose a reliable Wi-Fi network, enter the password, and wait for the connection to be established. If you're setting up your iPhone in a location where Wi-Fi is unavailable, you can skip this step and use cellular data, but connecting to Wi-Fi is recommended for a smoother setup experience.

4. Setting Up Face ID

One of the defining features of the iPhone 16 series is Face ID, Apple's facial recognition technology. During setup, you'll be asked if you want to configure Face ID. If you choose to enable it, you'll be guided through a process that involves positioning your face in front of the front-facing camera and slowly turning your head to capture multiple angles. This ensures that Face ID can recognize you from various perspectives.

Face ID is used not only to unlock your phone but also for secure authentication in apps and Apple Pay. If you prefer not to use Face ID, you can skip this step and set up a passcode instead. However, Face ID offers a higher level of security and convenience, making it worth the setup.

5. Creating or Signing into an Apple ID

An Apple ID is essential for using most of the iPhone's features, including downloading apps, syncing with iCloud, and using services like Apple Music and iMessage. During setup, you'll be prompted to either sign in with your existing Apple ID or create a new one.

- If you already have an Apple ID, simply enter your email address and password. You may also be asked to verify your identity using two-factor authentication if it's enabled.

- If you're new to Apple, you can create a new Apple ID by entering your email address, creating a password, and answering a few security questions.

Once signed in, your Apple ID will be linked to your iPhone, allowing you to sync your apps, contacts, and settings from iCloud if applicable.

6. Restoring from Backup or Setting Up as New

If you're upgrading from a previous iPhone or switching from an Android device, you'll have the option to restore your data from a backup. This allows you to transfer all your apps, settings, and personal data to your new iPhone without starting from scratch.

- Restore from iCloud Backup: If you've been using iCloud to back up your old iPhone, you can restore your data directly during setup. Simply sign in with your Apple ID and choose the most recent backup. Your iPhone will download the backup and restore your settings, apps, and data automatically.

- Restore from iTunes/Finder: If you've backed up your old iPhone to your computer using iTunes or Finder, you can restore from there. Connect your new iPhone to your computer via the USB-C to lightning cable and select "Restore from Backup" in iTunes or Finder.

- Transfer from Android: If you're switching from an Android device, Apple offers a "Move to iOS" app that makes transferring data simple. Download the app on your Android phone, and during the iPhone setup process, choose "Move Data from Android." Follow the on-screen instructions to transfer your contacts, messages, photos, and more.

If you prefer to set up your iPhone as a new device without transferring data, you can skip the restore options and start fresh.

Transferring Data from Old iPhone or Android

Apple has made it easy to transfer data from an old iPhone or even an Android device using several methods. Here are the most common options:

1. Quick Start

If you're upgrading from an older iPhone, Quick Start is the easiest way to transfer your data. With this feature, you can use your existing iPhone to set up your new device wirelessly. Here's how it works:

- Place your old iPhone near your new iPhone 16.
- A Quick Start screen will appear on your old iPhone, prompting you to confirm the transfer.
- Follow the on-screen instructions on both devices to connect them wirelessly.
- Your new iPhone will use the same Apple ID, and you can transfer your apps, data, and settings.

Quick Start is fast and efficient, allowing you to get your new iPhone up and running with minimal effort.

2. iCloud Backup

If you've been backing up your old iPhone to iCloud, you can use this backup to restore your data. Here's how to do it:

- During the setup process, choose "Restore from iCloud Backup."
- Sign in with your Apple ID.
- Select the most recent backup from your old iPhone.
- Your iPhone will download the backup, including your apps, data, and settings.

This method is especially useful if your old iPhone is no longer in your possession, as you can still access your data from iCloud.

3. Move to iOS (for Android Users)

For users switching from Android, Apple offers the "Move to iOS" app, which simplifies the process of transferring data. To use this option:

- Download the Move to iOS app from the Google Play Store on your Android device.
- During the iPhone setup process, choose "Move Data from Android."
- Open the Move to iOS app on your Android phone and follow the instructions to connect the devices.
- You can transfer contacts, message history, photos, videos, web bookmarks, and email accounts.

This option ensures that even Android users can switch to the iPhone 16 with ease.

Important Settings to Configure Immediately

Once your iPhone is set up and ready to use, there are several important settings that you should configure right away to ensure the best experience. These settings help protect your privacy and optimize the functionality of your new iPhone 16. By adjusting these critical settings from the start, you'll ensure that your device is secure, personalized, and performing at its best.

1. Privacy Settings

Apple is known for prioritizing user privacy, and the iPhone 16 offers a robust set of privacy tools to give you control over your data. Here are the most important privacy settings you should configure:

- **App Tracking Transparency:** One of the standout features in iOS is the ability to control which apps can track your activity across other websites and apps. This feature is essential for maintaining your privacy. When prompted, choose to allow or deny tracking for specific apps. You can also manage this setting in Settings > Privacy & Security > Tracking. It's recommended to deny tracking for most apps unless there's a specific reason to allow it.

- Location Services: You can control which apps have access to your location and when they are allowed to use it. For privacy and battery life optimization, go to Settings > Privacy & Security > Location Services and adjust location access for individual apps. You can choose between "Never," "Ask Next Time," "While Using the App," or "Always." For most apps, "While Using the App" is the safest and most battery-friendly option.

- Photo and Camera Access: Some apps may request access to your photos and camera. Go to Settings > Privacy & Security > Photos and Settings > Privacy & Security > Camera to control which apps can access these features. You can limit access to specific photos, which is a great way to maintain privacy without blocking app functionality entirely.

- Microphone and Bluetooth: Review which apps have access to your microphone and Bluetooth in Settings > Privacy & Security > Microphone and Settings > Privacy & Security > Bluetooth. For apps that don't need these features, it's best to disable access to reduce potential privacy risks.

2. Face ID and Passcode Setup

Security is a top priority, and enabling Face ID provides an additional layer of protection for your iPhone 16. If you skipped the Face ID setup during the initial configuration, you can enable it later in Settings > Face ID & Passcode. This feature uses advanced facial recognition technology to unlock your phone, authorize app purchases, and authenticate access to various services like Apple Pay.

Additionally, it's crucial to set a strong passcode as a backup to Face ID. Go to Settings > Face ID & Passcode to configure your passcode. Choose a six-digit passcode for optimal security, but you can also opt for a custom alphanumeric code if you want a more complex passcode.

3. Apple ID and iCloud Settings

Your Apple ID is central to your iPhone experience, linking all of your Apple devices and services together. After signing in with your Apple ID during setup, it's important to review your iCloud settings to ensure your data is synced and backed up properly.

- **iCloud Backup:** Automatic backups to iCloud are essential to protect your data in case something happens to your phone. To ensure backups are enabled, go to Settings > [Your Name] > iCloud > iCloud Backup. Toggle the switch to enable automatic backups. This way, your device will back up every time it's connected to Wi-Fi, charging, and locked.

- **iCloud Storage:** If you're using iCloud to store photos, documents, and other data, it's a good idea to check how much storage you have available. Free iCloud accounts come with 5GB of storage, but you can upgrade to a higher plan if needed. You can manage your iCloud storage by going to Settings > [Your Name] > iCloud > Manage Storage.

4. Siri and Voice Control

Siri, Apple's virtual assistant, is a powerful tool for hands-free interaction with your iPhone 16. To customize how Siri works for you, head to Settings > Siri & Search. Here, you can configure:

- **Listen for "Hey Siri":** Toggle this on to activate Siri by saying "Hey Siri" without needing to press any buttons.

- **Press Side Button for Siri:** This allows you to summon Siri by pressing and holding the side button.

- **Allow Siri When Locked:** Decide if you want Siri to be accessible when your phone is locked for quick access.

In addition to Siri, iOS 17 includes powerful voice control features. This feature allows you to use voice commands to control your iPhone, which can be helpful in certain situations. You can enable Voice

Control by going to Settings > Accessibility > Voice Control.

5. Apple Pay Setup

Apple Pay allows you to make secure payments with your iPhone at stores, within apps, and on websites. To set up Apple Pay, go to Settings > Wallet & Apple Pay. Follow the on-screen instructions to add your credit or debit cards by scanning them or entering the details manually. Apple Pay is not only a convenient feature, but it also adds a layer of security since your actual card details are never shared with merchants.

6. Focus Mode and Notifications

The iPhone 16 offers advanced notification management tools, including Focus Mode, which helps you minimize distractions by filtering notifications based on your current activity. Focus Modes can be customized for work, sleep, personal time, and more.

- **Customizing Focus Modes:** Go to Settings > Focus to set up different Focus profiles. For each mode, you can choose which apps and people are allowed to send notifications, as well as customize the Home Screen and Lock Screen to match the mode.

- **Notification Summaries:** iOS 17 introduces the ability to schedule Notification Summaries, which bundles non-urgent notifications and delivers them at a scheduled time. This keeps your Lock Screen uncluttered and helps you focus on the most important notifications. Set this up in Settings > Notifications > Scheduled Summary.

7. Emergency SOS and Medical ID

Your iPhone 16 includes several safety features that you should configure immediately. These settings can be life-saving in emergencies.

- **Emergency SOS:** Enable this feature in Settings > Emergency SOS. When enabled, you can press and hold the side button and one of the volume buttons to quickly call emergency services. You can also add emergency contacts, who will be notified of your location when you trigger SOS.

- **Medical ID:** In Settings > Health > Medical ID, you can fill in important medical information such as allergies, blood type, and emergency contacts. This information can be accessed from the Lock Screen by emergency responders, even if your phone is locked.

8. Display and Brightness Settings

The iPhone 16 series comes with the stunning Super Retina XDR display, which offers customizable brightness and color settings to suit your preferences. You can adjust these settings in Settings > Display & Brightness:

- **True Tone:** Enable True Tone to automatically adjust the display's color balance based on ambient lighting. This makes the screen easier on the eyes and provides a more natural viewing experience.

- **Dark Mode:** You can toggle Dark Mode on or off manually, or set it to activate automatically at sunset or a custom time. Dark Mode not only reduces eye strain in low-light environments but also helps conserve battery life on OLED screens like those on the iPhone 16.

- Auto-Lock: Customize the amount of time before your iPhone automatically locks when inactive. Go to Settings > Display & Brightness > Auto-Lock to choose the interval. Setting it to a shorter time helps preserve battery life and improves security.

9. Backup and Storage Management

Ensuring your data is safely backed up and that you have sufficient storage space is crucial for long-term performance and peace of mind. As mentioned earlier, enabling iCloud Backup is important, but you should also periodically check your device's local storage.

- Manage Storage: Go to Settings > General > iPhone Storage to view how much space is being used by apps, photos, messages, and other data. You can offload unused apps, clear temporary files, or purchase additional iCloud storage if needed.

- Optimize Photos Storage: If you take a lot of photos and videos, your storage may fill up quickly. In Settings > Photos, enable "Optimize iPhone Storage." This stores full-resolution images and videos in iCloud while keeping lower-resolution versions on your device to save space.

10. Automatic Software Updates

Finally, it's important to ensure that your iPhone 16 is always running the latest version of iOS. Apple regularly releases updates that include new features, security patches, and performance improvements. To enable automatic updates, go to Settings > General > Software Update > Automatic Updates and toggle on "Download iOS Updates" and "Install iOS Updates." This way, your device will automatically update overnight when it's charging and connected to Wi-Fi.

With your iPhone 16 unboxed and these critical settings configured, your device is now ready to deliver its full potential. This first-time setup process is designed to ensure your iPhone is optimized for performance, security, and user experience. From privacy settings and Face ID to Apple Pay and Focus Modes, your iPhone 16 is now tailored to your needs and preferences, providing a seamless experience from day one.

As you continue using your iPhone 16, you'll discover even more features and tools that will enhance your daily interactions with the device. By setting a strong foundation with these initial configurations, you can enjoy a smarter, safer, and more personalized smartphone experience.

CHAPTER 2

NAVIGATING THE IPHONE 16

*****

The iPhone 16 introduces several refinements to Apple's user interface, designed to provide a seamless and intuitive experience for users of all levels. With its clean, modern design, the iPhone 16 offers easy access to everything you need—from apps and widgets to multitasking tools and shortcuts. In this chapter, we'll explore the iPhone 16's user interface in depth, including the Lock Screen, Home Screen, and Control Center. We'll also cover gestures and shortcuts to enhance your productivity and provide tips on using widgets and managing your apps effectively with the App Library.

User Interface Overview

Apple has always been known for its polished, user-friendly design, and the iPhone 16 continues that tradition with subtle yet impactful improvements. The user interface is both simple and powerful, offering a visually appealing layout that prioritizes ease of use while giving you quick access to essential functions.

The Lock Screen

The Lock Screen is the first thing you see when you wake up your iPhone 16. Its primary function is to display time, notifications, and any personalized information you want to see at a glance, all while keeping your device secure. You can quickly access important features from the Lock Screen without having to unlock your phone.

Here's what you'll find on the Lock Screen:

1. Time and Date: Centered at the top, the time and date are prominently displayed in a clear, easy-to-read font. You can customize the font style and color from the Settings menu under Settings > Display & Brightness.

2. Notifications: Incoming notifications from apps and messages appear on the Lock Screen. You can swipe up to view more detailed notifications or swipe left on individual notifications to reveal options like clearing or responding to them. The iPhone 16 introduces improved notification grouping, so related notifications are bundled together, reducing clutter.

3. Quick Access to Camera and Flashlight: On the bottom corners of the Lock Screen, you'll see two icons: one for the camera and one for the flashlight. Pressing and holding these icons allows you to quickly open the camera or turn on the flashlight without unlocking your device.

4. Face ID and Security: As you glance at your iPhone 16, Face ID will automatically authenticate you and unlock the device. This makes transitioning from the Lock Screen to the Home Screen faster and more seamless than ever before. For added security, your notifications can be hidden on the Lock Screen until Face ID recognizes you, ensuring your privacy.

The Home Screen

Once you unlock your phone, the Home Screen is where you'll spend much of your time. Apple has refined the Home Screen layout on the iPhone 16 to offer better customization and smoother transitions between apps.

Key elements of the Home Screen include:

1. App Icons: Apps are arranged in a grid-like format across multiple pages. You can organize apps into folders by dragging one app on top of another, creating clusters for productivity, social media, or entertainment. You can also adjust the app grid by holding down an empty area on the Home Screen until the apps jiggle, allowing you to rearrange them.

2. Dock: Located at the bottom of the screen, the Dock holds your most frequently used apps. It remains static, even as you swipe between different Home Screen pages, making it easy to access key apps like Messages, Safari, or Music at any time.

3. Search Bar: At the bottom of the Home Screen, you'll notice a small Search bar, represented by a magnifying glass icon. Swipe down on the screen, and you'll activate Spotlight Search, which lets you search for apps, contacts, messages, files, and even web results. The search feature is lightning-fast, making it a go-to tool for finding what you need quickly.

4. App Library: Swiping to the right will bring you to the App Library. This is a smart organizational system that automatically categorizes all your apps into folders like Suggestions, Recently Added, Social, and Entertainment. It's designed to reduce the clutter of multiple Home Screen pages and offer easy access to apps you don't use frequently.

The Control Center

The Control Center is a powerful tool that allows you to manage key functions of your iPhone 16 with just a few swipes. Accessible by swiping down from the top-right corner of the screen, the Control Center includes shortcuts to essential features like Wi-Fi, Bluetooth, screen brightness, and music playback.

Here's a closer look at the Control Center's layout:

1. Connectivity Options: At the top-left corner, you'll find toggles for Wi-Fi, Bluetooth, and Airplane Mode. Long-pressing these icons gives you access to additional settings, such as connecting to specific Wi-Fi networks or Bluetooth devices.

2. Media Playback: Below the connectivity options, you'll find a media playback section that allows you to control music, podcasts, or video playback. You can play, pause, skip tracks, and adjust the volume directly from the Control Center without opening the specific app.

3. Brightness and Volume Sliders: Adjusting the screen brightness and system volume is as simple as dragging the sliders up or down. For more granular control, long-press on these sliders to reveal additional options, such as turning on Night Shift or adjusting Spatial Audio settings when using AirPods Pro.

4. Additional Tools: The Control Center also includes quick-access buttons for features like the flashlight, screen mirroring, and Do Not Disturb mode. These can be customized in Settings > Control Center, where you can add or remove tools based on your preferences.

Gestures and Shortcuts

Apple's focus on gesture-based navigation in recent iPhone models continues with the iPhone 16, making multitasking and moving between apps more fluid and intuitive. In this section, we'll explore the key gestures and shortcuts that make using your iPhone 16 a smooth experience.

Key Gestures

1. Home Gesture: Since the removal of the physical Home button, returning to the Home Screen is done via a simple swipe. From any app, swipe up from the bottom of the screen to return to the Home Screen. This gesture becomes second nature quickly, eliminating the need for buttons.

2. App Switching: Switching between apps is faster than ever on the iPhone 16. Swipe up from the bottom of the screen and hold your finger in place for a second to bring up the app switcher. You can then swipe left or right to browse through your recently used apps. Alternatively, you can swipe along the bottom edge of the screen to quickly jump between apps without bringing up the app switcher.

3. Control Center Access: As mentioned earlier, swiping down from the top-right corner of the screen opens the Control Center. This gesture is ideal for quickly adjusting settings without interrupting what you're doing.

4. Notification Center Access: Swiping down from the top-left corner of the screen reveals the Notification Center. This is where you can view and manage notifications, such as missed calls, text messages, or app alerts.

5. Screenshot and Screen Recording: Taking a screenshot is as simple as pressing the side button and the volume up button at the same time. If you want to record your screen, you can add the Screen Recording option to the Control Center through Settings > Control Center. Once it's added, you can start recording by tapping the Screen Recording icon.

6. Reachability: The iPhone 16's large screen can make it difficult to reach the top of the display with one hand. To help with this, Apple has a feature called Reachability. You can enable this in Settings > Accessibility > Touch > Reachability. Once enabled, swipe down on the bottom edge of the screen, and the top half of the display will slide down, making it easier to reach icons and buttons.

Multitasking Features

The iPhone 16 excels at multitasking, making it easy to switch between apps or perform multiple tasks at once. Here are some multitasking features to take advantage of:

1. Slide Over: Although primarily seen on iPads, the iPhone 16 also offers a form of split-screen multitasking known as Slide Over. When using apps like Safari or Notes, you can swipe in from the side to bring another app into view without fully switching apps. This makes it easy to reference information from one app while working on another.

2. Picture-in-Picture (PiP): The Picture-in-Picture feature allows you to continue watching videos or taking FaceTime calls while using other apps. When watching a video, swipe up to go to the Home Screen, and the video will shrink into a floating window that can be moved around. This feature is perfect for multitasking, such as responding to messages while watching YouTube.

Keyboard Shortcuts

Typing on the iPhone 16 is faster and more customizable than ever. The built-in keyboard has received several improvements, including better autocorrect, predictive text, and new shortcuts.

1. QuickPath Typing: Apple's swipe-based typing method, known as QuickPath, allows you to type by sliding your finger from one letter to the next without lifting it off the keyboard. This speeds up typing, especially for one-handed use, and is great for composing messages quickly.

2. Shortcut Bar: At the top of the keyboard, you'll find a shortcut bar that offers suggestions based on what you're typing. This bar provides quick access to emojis, punctuation, and other predictive text options. You can customize the bar by adding frequently used symbols and commands.

3. Text Replacement: You can create custom keyboard shortcuts for phrases you type often by going to Settings > General > Keyboard > Text Replacement. For example, you could set up "omw" to automatically expand to "On my way!" when typed. This is a handy time-saver for commonly used phrases.

4. Dictation: For hands-free typing, tap the microphone icon on the keyboard and dictate your message. The iPhone 16's improved dictation feature uses the Neural Engine to understand natural speech better and punctuate sentences automatically, making voice input more accurate and faster.

Widgets and App Library

Widgets and the App Library are powerful tools for organizing your Home Screen and keeping everything within easy reach. Apple has continued to refine these features, giving users even more control over how they interact with their apps and information.

Using Widgets Effectively

Widgets allow you to place live information from your favorite apps directly on your Home Screen. From weather updates to calendar events, widgets provide at-a-glance data without needing to open the app.

1. Adding Widgets: To add a widget, press and hold a space on the Home Screen until the apps start jiggling. Tap the + button in the top-left corner to open the widget gallery, where you can browse and choose from a variety of widget sizes and designs.

2. Smart Stacks: Smart Stacks are a special type of widget that dynamically changes throughout the day based on your usage patterns. For example, in the morning, it might show the news, and in the evening, it could display your fitness activity. You can customize Smart Stacks by swiping through different widgets or pressing and holding the stack to edit its contents.

3. Widget Size and Placement: Widgets come in three sizes: small, medium, and large. Choose the size that fits your Home Screen layout and your needs. For instance, a small weather widget might fit perfectly in the top corner of your Home Screen, while a large calendar widget can take up more space if you need to view your schedule at a glance.

4. Interactive Widgets: The iPhone 16 introduces interactive widgets that allow you to perform tasks directly from the widget itself. For example, you can control music playback, check off reminders, or adjust smart home settings without opening the corresponding app.

Managing Apps in the App Library

The App Library is an organizational feature that automatically sorts your apps into categorized folders, making it easier to find the apps you use less frequently.

1. Accessing the App Library: Swipe to the rightmost page on your Home Screen to access the App Library. You'll see your apps organized into categories such as Social, Entertainment, Creativity, and more. The top section of the App Library features Suggestions and Recently Added apps for quick access to apps you use often or have just downloaded.

2. Using the Search Bar: At the top of the App Library, you'll find a search bar. You can type the name of the app you're looking for, or you can scroll through the alphabetical list of all installed apps.

3. Hiding Home Screen Pages: If you prefer to keep your Home Screen clutter-free, you can hide entire pages of apps and rely solely on the App Library. To hide a page, press and hold on a blank area of the Home Screen, then tap the page dots at the bottom of the screen. You'll enter Edit Pages mode, where you can uncheck any Home Screen pages you want to hide.

4. Organizing Your Apps: Although the App Library automatically organizes your apps, you can also manually remove apps from the Home Screen while keeping them in the App Library. Press and hold an app icon, then select Remove App. Choose Move to App Library to keep the app accessible in the library without cluttering your Home Screen.

By leveraging widgets and the App Library, you can create a clean, organized, and highly functional Home Screen that adapts to your needs throughout the day.

With the iPhone 16, Apple has refined the user interface to offer a smoother, more intuitive experience that balances simplicity with powerful multitasking tools. By mastering the Lock Screen, Home Screen, and Control Center, you'll gain faster access to your favorite apps and settings. The gestures and shortcuts introduced with the iPhone 16 further enhance productivity, while widgets and the App Library allow you to customize your Home Screen in a way that's both functional and aesthetically pleasing.

As you explore the various features outlined in this chapter, you'll find that the iPhone 16 is designed to adapt to your unique workflow, making everyday tasks easier, more efficient, and more enjoyable.

CHAPTER 3

CUSTOMIZATION

*****

One of the most exciting aspects of using an iPhone is the ability to personalize it according to your preferences and needs. With the iPhone 16, Apple has expanded customization options even further, giving users a highly flexible and powerful toolkit to make their devices truly their own. From rearranging apps and adding widgets to enabling Dark Mode and managing notifications, customization on the iPhone 16 allows you to create a user experience that is both aesthetically pleasing and functionally efficient. In this chapter, we'll dive deep into the various customization options available and walk you through the steps to make your iPhone 16 a reflection of your style and workflow.

Customizing the Home Screen

The Home Screen is the central hub of your iPhone, and Apple has made it easier than ever to organize apps, create folders, and add widgets to ensure that everything is exactly where you want it. Let's go through the process of Home Screen customization step by step.

1. Rearranging Apps

Organizing your apps is one of the simplest ways to make your Home Screen more functional. By rearranging app icons, you can place the most frequently used apps within easy reach and create a logical flow that suits your daily routine.

- **To move an app:** Tap and hold on any app icon until a context menu appears. Select Edit Home Screen and all of the apps will start to jiggle. Now, simply drag the app to its new location on the screen. You can move it to a different spot on the same page, or swipe left or right to place it on a different Home Screen page.

- Creating folders: Grouping similar apps into folders is a great way to declutter your Home Screen. To create a folder, tap and hold on an app until the icons jiggle, then drag the app onto another app. This will automatically create a folder containing both apps. You can rename the folder by tapping the text at the top of the folder and entering a new name. Popular categories for folders include Social, Work, Entertainment, and Productivity.

- Moving apps to the Dock: The Dock is located at the bottom of the screen and holds up to four apps that are always accessible, no matter which page of your Home Screen you're on. To move an app to the Dock, follow the same process for rearranging apps. Simply drag the app from the Home Screen to the Dock.

- Removing apps: If you want to clean up your Home Screen further, you can remove apps without deleting them entirely. Tap and hold the app icon, select Remove App, and then choose Move to App Library. This keeps the app accessible from the App Library without cluttering your Home Screen.

2. Adding Widgets

Widgets are a powerful tool for customizing the Home Screen by giving you quick access to live information, such as weather updates, calendar events, or battery status. The iPhone 16 expands on this functionality, allowing for interactive widgets that can be updated in real time without needing to open the app.

- **To add a widget:** Tap and hold on a space on the Home Screen until the app icons start jiggling. Tap the + button in the top-left corner of the screen to open the widget gallery. Here, you can browse available widgets from different apps, choose from different sizes (small, medium, large), and select the one that suits your needs.

- **Customizing widgets:** Some widgets allow for further customization, such as choosing which information they display. For example, you can add a Weather widget and configure it to show the forecast for your current location or a specific city. To customize a widget, tap and hold it on the Home Screen, then select Edit Widget from the menu.

- Using Smart Stacks: Smart Stacks are dynamic widgets that rotate throughout the day based on your usage patterns. To add a Smart Stack, go to the widget gallery and choose Smart Stack. You can edit the Smart Stack by pressing and holding it, then selecting Edit Stack. From here, you can add or remove widgets within the stack or enable Smart Rotate to automatically change the displayed widget based on the time of day or activity.

- Widget placement: The placement of widgets is crucial to an efficient Home Screen layout. You can place widgets on their own or mix them with app icons. Drag widgets around the screen to find the ideal spot for quick access to important information. For example, placing a calendar widget at the top of the screen can help you keep track of your day at a glance.

Dark Mode and Appearance Settings

Customizing the appearance of your iPhone 16 goes beyond just the Home Screen layout. Apple has introduced a variety of display settings that allow you to adjust the look and feel of the interface. Dark Mode, True Tone, and Night Shift are three key features that can transform the way your iPhone looks and how comfortable it is to use in different lighting conditions.

1. Enabling Dark Mode

Dark Mode is a popular feature that changes the entire system interface to a darker color scheme. It's not just a cosmetic change—it can also reduce eye strain in low-light environments and conserve battery life on the iPhone 16's OLED screen.

- To enable Dark Mode manually: Go to Settings > Display & Brightness, and under the Appearance section, select Dark. This will immediately switch the interface to Dark Mode. If you ever want to revert to the default light appearance, simply select Light in the same menu.

- Scheduling Dark Mode: If you want Dark Mode to automatically turn on at sunset and off at sunrise, toggle the Automatic option in Settings > Display & Brightness. You can also set a custom schedule by selecting Options under Automatic, allowing you to choose specific times for Dark Mode to activate.

- Dark Mode in apps: Many apps now support Dark Mode, automatically adjusting their color scheme when Dark Mode is enabled on the system. Whether you're using native Apple apps like Mail, Safari, and Messages or third-party apps, the majority of apps will follow the system's Dark Mode setting for a more consistent user experience.

2. Customizing Display Settings: True Tone and Night Shift

In addition to Dark Mode, Apple offers other display features that improve your viewing experience based on the surrounding environment.

- True Tone: True Tone uses the iPhone's ambient light sensor to adjust the display's color temperature based on the lighting around you. This helps make the screen more comfortable to look at, as it mimics the natural lighting environment. To enable or disable True Tone, go to Settings > Display & Brightness, and toggle True Tone on or off. You can also adjust this setting from the Control Center by long-pressing the brightness slider.

- **Night Shift:** Night Shift reduces the amount of blue light emitted by the screen, making the display appear warmer. Blue light is known to interfere with sleep patterns, so enabling Night Shift can help reduce eye strain and promote better sleep if you're using your iPhone late at night. To enable Night Shift, go to Settings > Display & Brightness > Night Shift. From here, you can manually turn on the Night Shift or schedule it to activate at a specific time, such as from sunset to sunrise. You can also adjust the warmth of the display to suit your comfort level.

By combining Dark Mode, True Tone, and Night Shift, you can create a display environment that is not only visually appealing but also reduces strain on your eyes and adapts to various lighting conditions throughout the day.

Notification Management

With the growing number of apps and services on your iPhone, managing notifications has become more important than ever. The iPhone 16 introduces enhanced notification management tools, allowing you to control when and how you receive alerts. Customizing these settings helps reduce distractions and ensures that you only receive the most important notifications when you need them.

1. Focus Modes

Focus Modes are one of the standout features for managing notifications on the iPhone 16. Focus Modes allow you to create custom profiles that limit notifications and alerts based on the activity you're engaged in. Whether you're working, relaxing, or sleeping, Focus Modes help you filter out distractions and stay focused on the task at hand.

- **Setting up Focus Modes:** Go to Settings > Focus, and you'll see several pre-configured Focus profiles, such as Do Not Disturb, Work, and Sleep. Tap on any of these profiles to customize their settings, or create a new Focus Mode by tapping the + button.

- Customizing a Focus Mode: For each Focus profile, you can choose which apps and contacts are allowed to send you notifications while the mode is active. For example, during Work mode, you might allow notifications from messaging apps like Slack but block social media alerts. Additionally, you can customize the Home Screen and Lock Screen pages to match each Focus Mode, showing only the apps you need for that specific activity.

- Automatic activation: Focus Modes can be set to turn on automatically based on time, location, or app usage. For instance, you can have Sleep mode activate automatically at 10 PM every night, or Work mode turn on when you arrive at your office. This feature is perfect for those who want to maintain a seamless routine without constantly adjusting settings.

- Sharing Focus Status: When you enable a Focus Mode, you can choose to share your Focus Status with contacts in apps like Messages. This lets people know that you have notifications silenced and may not respond immediately, helping manage expectations without cutting off communication completely.

2. Customizing Notifications

In addition to Focus Modes, iOS 17 offers powerful tools for customizing how and when you receive notifications. You can control which apps send notifications, how they appear on the screen, and even when they are delivered.

- **App-specific notifications:** To customize notifications for individual apps, go to Settings > Notifications. Here, you'll see a list of all your installed apps. Select any app to adjust its notification settings, including the type of alert (banner, sound, or badge) and whether notifications are allowed to appear on the Lock Screen or Notification Center. You can also choose whether to show previews of notifications or hide sensitive information until Face ID unlocks the phone.

- **Scheduled Summary:** The Scheduled Summary feature lets you bundle non-urgent notifications and deliver them at a specific time of your choosing. This keeps your Lock Screen clean throughout the day while ensuring you don't miss important updates. To enable a Scheduled Summary, go to Settings > Notifications > Scheduled Summary and choose the apps you want to include. You can then set delivery times, such as morning and evening, to receive a summary of all the notifications you've missed.

- **Grouping notifications:** iOS automatically groups related notifications to reduce clutter. In Settings > Notifications, you can choose between Automatic (the default), By App (groups all notifications from the same app), or Off (displays each notification individually). Grouping notifications by app is a great way to keep related messages and alerts together, especially for messaging or social media apps.

- **Sound and vibration settings:** For each app, you can customize the notification sound or choose to disable sound and rely solely on visual alerts. You can also adjust vibration patterns for incoming notifications by going to Settings > Sounds & Haptics.

3. Managing Alerts

Some notifications require immediate attention, such as phone calls or emergency alerts. The iPhone 16 allows you to manage critical alerts separately from other notifications.

- **Emergency Alerts:** Go to Settings > Notifications > Government Alerts to control whether emergency alerts like AMBER Alerts, weather warnings, or public safety alerts are delivered to your iPhone. These alerts can be crucial, so it's generally a good idea to keep them enabled.

- **Phone and Message Alerts:** You can set specific notification preferences for phone calls and messages by going to Settings > Phone and Settings > Messages. Here, you can adjust whether you want incoming calls and texts to bypass certain Focus Modes, ensuring that critical communication always gets through.

By carefully managing notifications, you can minimize distractions and keep your iPhone 16 optimized for the things that matter most. Whether you rely on Focus Modes to limit interruptions or customize individual app notifications for greater control, the tools available in iOS 17 make it easier than ever to manage alerts on your terms.

Customization on the iPhone 16 is about more than just aesthetics; it's about creating a user experience that fits seamlessly into your life. From organizing your Home Screen with apps and widgets to customizing the display settings for comfort and style, the iPhone 16 provides an array of options that allow you to tailor the device to your personal preferences.

By mastering notification management and using Focus Modes to stay productive, you'll also gain control over how your iPhone interacts with you throughout the day. With the wealth of customization options available, your iPhone 16 can become an extension of your workflow, helping you stay organized, focused, and in control at all times.

CHAPTER 4

iOS 17 FEATURES

*****

The introduction of iOS 17 brings a wave of powerful and refined features designed to make the iPhone 16 experience even more dynamic, personalized, and secure. With an emphasis on privacy, enhanced usability, and deeper interactivity, iOS 17 transforms how users interact with their devices. From new privacy settings to more versatile widgets and improvements to core apps like iMessage, Apple's latest operating system continues to build on the strengths of its predecessors while introducing exciting innovations that cater to both casual users and tech enthusiasts alike.

Overview of iOS 17

iOS 17 is packed with enhancements and new functionalities, making it one of the most versatile iOS updates yet. Apple has focused on improving the core user experience by enhancing existing features, adding new ones, and giving users greater control over their devices. Below are some of the most notable features introduced in iOS 17.

1. Enhanced Privacy Settings

In today's digital world, privacy is more important than ever, and iOS 17 doubles down on Apple's commitment to user privacy. One of the standout privacy features in iOS 17 is App Privacy Reports. This tool gives users a detailed overview of how apps are using their permissions, including how often apps access sensitive information such as location, photos, camera, microphone, and contacts. By visiting Settings > Privacy & Security > App Privacy Report, users can review this data and adjust app permissions accordingly, providing full transparency and control over how personal information is used.

Another key addition is Mail Privacy Protection, which prevents senders from tracking when and where you open an email. This feature blocks invisible tracking pixels often embedded in marketing emails, stopping companies from collecting your data without consent. You can enable this in Settings > Mail > Privacy Protection.

Lastly, Private Relay continues to evolve, offering even stronger online privacy when browsing in Safari. This iCloud+ feature encrypts your internet traffic, preventing websites and advertisers from tracking your browsing activity across the web. When enabled, Private Relay hides your IP address and location, making it harder for sites to build a profile on your habits.

2. Redesigned Widgets and Lock Screen Customization

Widgets have become more functional and interactive in iOS 17. While widgets were first introduced to the Home Screen in iOS 14, iOS 17 takes them a step further by making them interactive. This means you can perform tasks directly from the widget itself without needing to open the app. Whether you're marking off reminders, controlling music playback, or adjusting smart home settings, interactive widgets offer a seamless way to manage tasks.

The Lock Screen in iOS 17 is also more customizable than ever. You can now add widgets to the Lock Screen, making important information accessible at a glance without unlocking your phone. In addition to weather and calendar widgets, you can include widgets for health metrics, news updates, and fitness goals, all in a layout that suits your preferences.

3. Updated Safari Experience

Safari gets a significant boost in iOS 17 with improvements aimed at enhancing browsing speed, security, and organization. One of the most useful features is Shared Tab Groups, which lets you share entire tab groups with others, making collaboration on projects or trip planning easier. You can also leave comments and tag specific tabs for better communication within the shared group.

Face ID is now supported within Safari to protect sensitive content, such as passwords and saved login credentials, behind biometric authentication. Additionally, Safari Extensions are more widely available, enabling users to customize their browsing experience with added functionality like ad blockers, password managers, and more.

4. New AirDrop Features

AirDrop remains one of the most convenient ways to share files, photos, and links between Apple devices, and iOS 17 introduces new features that make AirDrop even better. Contact Posters is a standout feature that lets you personalize how your contact information appears when sharing via AirDrop. You can customize your Contact Poster with a photo, Memoji, or custom font, and it will display whenever you share contact details with others.

Additionally, NameDrop is a new AirDrop feature that makes it easier to share contact information. By simply holding two iPhones close together, users can instantly share their name, phone number, and email address without needing to manually enter the information.

AirDrop in iOS 17 also supports larger file transfers that can continue even after you walk away from the recipient. If you're in the middle of sharing a large video or photo album and need to leave, iOS will complete the transfer via iCloud, ensuring you don't lose progress.

5. Siri and AI Enhancements

Siri in iOS 17 benefits from more refined natural language processing and improved AI-based suggestions. Instead of needing to say "Hey Siri" to activate the voice assistant, iOS 17 allows users to simply say "Siri," making interactions faster and more streamlined. Siri also now supports back-to-back commands, so you can issue multiple requests without needing to reactivate Siri after each one.

AI-based suggestions are also present throughout the operating system, with Siri offering more intelligent and relevant recommendations based on your habits and location. For example, Siri might suggest putting your phone into Do Not Disturb mode if it recognizes that you're in a meeting, or recommend a playlist when you arrive at the gym.

6. Real-Time Live Activities

Live Activities in iOS 17 provide users with real-time updates directly on the Lock Screen. This feature is especially useful for tracking time-sensitive events like food deliveries, sports scores, or ride-sharing services. For example, if you're waiting for an Uber or Lyft, the status of your ride will be displayed in real-time on the Lock Screen, complete with the driver's ETA, car details, and route progress.

Live Activities are customizable, and developers can integrate them into their apps. This means you can stay up-to-date on important tasks or events without needing to open the relevant app. You can enable or adjust Live Activities for each app in Settings > Notifications > Live Activities.

New iMessage Features

iMessage, Apple's default messaging app, has been a cornerstone of iOS for years. With iOS 17, iMessage has received a significant overhaul, introducing several new features that make communicating more fun, expressive, and interactive.

1. Stickers and Emoji Reactions

Stickers in iMessage have been revamped to become a more central part of the messaging experience. You can now create custom stickers from photos or Memoji and use them to react to messages in real-time. Stickers are no longer limited to the iMessage app store—any photo or image can be turned into a sticker that you can send or use to decorate chat threads.

Emoji reactions have also been improved, allowing for more nuanced and expressive communication. Instead of just sending a basic thumbs-up or heart, users can now attach emojis directly to specific words or phrases in a message, offering a more personal and playful way to respond.

2. Audio Message Transcriptions

iMessage in iOS 17 now automatically transcribes audio messages. This feature is particularly useful for users who receive voice messages but may be in situations where they cannot listen to them immediately, such as in a meeting or a quiet environment. The transcription appears directly in the chat, allowing you to read the message at your convenience while keeping the original audio available for later listening.

3. Group Chats and Inline Replies

Group chats in iMessage have also seen improvements. One of the key new features is inline replies, which lets you respond directly to a specific message in a group conversation. This is especially useful in large group chats where conversations can become chaotic. With inline replies, users can maintain clearer, more focused conversations within the larger chat, reducing confusion.

Another enhancement is the @mentions feature. Similar to popular messaging apps like Slack, you can now type @username to grab someone's attention in a busy group chat. When mentioned, the user will receive a specific notification, ensuring they don't miss important messages.

4. AI-Based Suggestions

Apple has integrated AI-based suggestions into iMessage, providing users with smart replies based on the context of the conversation. For example, if someone asks for your location, iMessage might suggest sharing your current location directly from the conversation window. If you're discussing a plan, the AI might recommend sending an event invite or scheduling a reminder.

These AI-based suggestions are context-aware, meaning they evolve based on your usage patterns, making messaging more efficient and less time-consuming.

Interactive Widgets

iOS 17's interactive widgets represent one of the most significant updates to the Home Screen experience. While widgets were originally introduced to display passive information, such as weather forecasts or calendar events, interactive widgets let you perform actions directly from the widget itself.

1. Task Management and Reminders

One of the most practical applications of interactive widgets is in task management. With iOS 17, you can now interact with a Reminders widget by marking tasks as complete or adding new ones directly from the Home Screen. This eliminates the need to open the app to update your to-do list, streamlining productivity.

For example, if you have a Smart Stack that includes a Reminders widget, you can swipe through the stack to check off tasks, add deadlines, or even adjust priorities, all from the widget itself. This is especially useful for users who rely on their iPhones for task management throughout the day.

2. Music and Media Control

Widgets in iOS 17 also enhance how you control media playback. With interactive widgets for Apple Music and other media apps, you can play, pause, skip tracks, and adjust the volume without needing to open the app. These widgets can be placed on your Home Screen for quick access, and they offer more flexibility than the Control Center alone.

For users

Who consume a lot of podcasts, music, or audiobooks, this new level of interactivity simplifies media control. Whether you're in the middle of a workout or commuting, you can quickly adjust your media playback with a single tap.

3. Calendar and Event Management

The Calendar widget is another standout in iOS 17's interactive widget lineup. Instead of simply displaying upcoming events, the interactive Calendar widget allows you to respond to event invitations, edit event details, or add new events directly from the widget. This feature is invaluable for busy professionals who rely on their iPhones to manage their schedules.

For example, if you're reminded of an upcoming meeting, you can tap on the Calendar widget to adjust the meeting time, add attendees, or check meeting notes without needing to open the full Calendar app. This not only saves time but also keeps your schedule more organized.

4. Home Automation

If you use Apple's Home app to manage smart devices, iOS 17's interactive widgets take home automation to the next level. Widgets for smart lights, thermostats, and security cameras allow you to control these devices directly from the Home Screen.

You can turn on the lights, adjust the thermostat, or check your front door camera with just a tap on the widget, making smart home management more accessible and efficient.

For those deeply integrated into the Apple Home ecosystem, the interactive widget feature simplifies daily routines and improves the overall smart home experience.

iOS 17 represents a major leap forward in customization, usability, and interactivity. From enhanced privacy controls to new iMessage features and the introduction of interactive widgets, this update ensures that the iPhone 16 remains at the cutting edge of mobile technology. By embracing these new features, users can expect a more personalized, secure, and efficient experience across their devices.

With tools like real-time Live Activities, AI-based suggestions, and intuitive widgets, iOS 17 transforms how users manage tasks, communicate, and interact with their apps. Whether you're a productivity-focused professional or someone who loves to customize every aspect of your device, iOS 17 brings new layers of functionality that can enhance every aspect of your digital life.

CHAPTER 5

USING THE CAMERA

*****

The iPhone 16 series comes equipped with some of the most advanced camera technology ever seen in a smartphone. Whether you're a professional photographer or simply enjoy capturing moments from your everyday life, the iPhone 16's camera system delivers exceptional quality and features that cater to a wide range of users. This chapter will take an in-depth look at the Pro Camera Features, explore photography tips for both casual users and professionals, and cover the advanced capabilities for video recording and editing. With the iPhone 16, iPhone 16 Pro, and iPhone 16 Pro Max, Apple has raised the bar once again for smartphone photography and videography.

Pro Camera Features

Apple's Pro Camera features on the iPhone 16 series bring the power of professional-grade photography and video capabilities into the hands of everyday users. Whether you're using the standard iPhone 16 or the high-end iPhone 16 Pro Max, these features allow for impressive flexibility and control, making the iPhone 16 series an excellent choice for those who want to capture stunning images and videos.

1. ProRAW and ProRes

The ProRAW and ProRes features are major selling points for professionals and enthusiasts alike, providing more control over image and video quality.

- **ProRAW:** The iPhone 16's ProRAW feature allows you to capture images in RAW format, which retains more data than a standard JPEG or HEIC image. This gives photographers more flexibility in post-processing, as they can adjust things like exposure, color balance, and shadows without losing image quality. While standard photos are processed automatically to optimize for brightness and contrast, ProRAW images give you the freedom to edit them in more detail. This is perfect for professional photographers who want more creative control over their shots.

To enable ProRAW, go to Settings > Camera > Formats and toggle on ProRAW. You can then choose to shoot in RAW by tapping the RAW button in the Camera app when taking photos.

- ProRes: For videographers, ProRes is a game-changing feature. It allows you to shoot video in the same high-quality format used in professional film production. ProRes video files retain more color information and dynamic range, making them ideal for editing in post-production software. While ProRes files are larger and require more storage space, they offer far greater flexibility for color grading and editing.

To enable ProRes, head to Settings > Camera > Formats and toggle on ProRes. When shooting video in the Camera app, you can select the ProRes option, which is ideal for capturing cinematic-quality video.

2. Cinematic Mode

Introduced with the iPhone 13, Cinematic Mode continues to evolve with the iPhone 16 series, allowing users to shoot video with a shallow depth of field, similar to what you'd find in professional cinema. Cinematic Mode automatically focuses on the subject of your video while artfully blurring the background, creating a more dynamic and visually appealing shot. What makes Cinematic Mode in the iPhone 16 even more impressive is the ability to change focus points after recording.

For instance, if you're filming a conversation between two people, Cinematic Mode can intelligently switch focus from one speaker to the other, keeping the scene fluid and engaging. After recording, you can adjust the focus points in the Photos or iMovie app, which adds to the flexibility of this feature.

To use Cinematic Mode, open the Camera app, swipe to Cinematic, and start recording. You'll notice that the camera automatically identifies subjects and adjusts focus accordingly. You can manually tap on different areas of the screen to change focus points while recording.

3. New Zoom Capabilities for Pro Max

The iPhone 16 Pro Max introduces a periscope-style telephoto lens, which offers up to 10x optical zoom—a first for iPhones. This allows users to capture distant subjects with incredible clarity and detail, making the Pro Max model ideal for landscape photography, sporting events, and wildlife photography.

While digital zoom has been available for years, it often results in a loss of image quality. The new optical zoom feature uses physical lens adjustments to maintain sharpness and clarity, even at maximum zoom levels. Combined with Apple's advanced computational photography algorithms, the iPhone 16 Pro Max can deliver stunning zoomed-in images that rival standalone cameras.

The camera system also supports digital zoom up to 25x, but for best results, the optical zoom options between 0.5x and 10x are preferred. To switch between zoom levels, simply tap the zoom controls in the Camera app, or pinch the screen to zoom in or out.

Photography Tips

The iPhone 16's camera system is packed with features that cater to both casual users and professionals. However, understanding how to use these tools effectively can make a big difference in the quality of your photos. Below are some photography tips and tricks to help you get the most out of your iPhone 16 camera.

1. Mastering Lighting

Lighting is one of the most important factors in photography, and the iPhone 16's camera excels in various lighting conditions. Here are a few tips to make the most of the available light:

- **Natural Light:** When shooting outdoors, try to take advantage of natural light. Early morning or late afternoon (referred to as "golden hour") provides the best lighting for capturing warm, soft shadows. Avoid shooting in harsh midday sunlight, which can create strong contrasts and overexposed highlights.

- Low-Light Photography: The iPhone 16 has a powerful Night Mode, which automatically activates in low-light conditions. Night Mode uses longer exposure times and advanced algorithms to capture more light, resulting in clear and detailed photos even in dim settings. To get the best results, hold your phone steady while Night Mode is active. You can also use a tripod for even more stability in very low-light environments.

- Using Artificial Light: When shooting indoors, avoid harsh artificial lighting like fluorescent lights, as they can cast unflattering colors on your subject. Instead, use soft, diffused light sources, such as lamps with shades or natural window light. If you're using the iPhone's flash, be mindful that the built-in flash works best in close-range scenarios.

2. Portrait Mode

Portrait Mode on the iPhone 16 allows you to capture photos with a beautifully blurred background (bokeh effect), which makes your subject stand out more clearly. This mode is perfect for taking professional-looking headshots, pet photos, or any image where you want to emphasize the subject.

- Choosing the Right Distance: Portrait Mode works best when your subject is positioned about 2-8 feet away from the camera. If you're too close or too far, the camera may struggle to create the desired depth effect.

- Lighting in Portrait Mode: Make sure your subject is well-lit. The camera uses the light on the subject to differentiate it from the background and create the bokeh effect. Poor lighting can cause the depth effect to look unnatural or uneven.

- Portrait Lighting Effects: Portrait Mode comes with various lighting effects like Studio Light, Contour Light, and Stage Light. Each effect creates a different mood by adjusting the lighting around your subject. Experiment with these effects by swiping through the options in the Camera app while using Portrait Mode.

3. Composition and Framing

Good composition can make or break a photograph. The iPhone 16 offers several tools to help you improve the composition of your shots:

- **Rule of Thirds:** Use the gridlines in the Camera app to apply the Rule of Thirds, which involves placing your subject along the gridlines or at the intersection points. This creates a more balanced and visually appealing image. To enable the grid, go to Settings > Camera > Grid.

- **Symmetry and Leading Lines:** Look for natural lines or symmetry in your environment to guide the viewer's eye toward your subject. Leading lines can be anything from roads, rivers, or fences that draw attention to the main focus of the photo.

- **Negative Space:** Don't be afraid to leave space around your subject. Negative space can create a sense of scale and make your subject stand out more effectively. For example, when photographing a person against a landscape, leaving open sky or horizon lines can make the image more striking.

4. Taking Advantage of HDR

HDR (High Dynamic Range) is a feature that enhances photos by balancing the exposure between the brightest and darkest areas of an image. The iPhone 16 uses Smart HDR 5, an updated version that uses AI to intelligently analyze and merge multiple exposures into one image with optimal lighting and detail.

HDR is especially useful in high-contrast situations, such as capturing a bright sky while keeping the foreground well-exposed. The feature is automatically enabled in most cases, but you can turn it off or adjust it manually by tapping the HDR icon in the Camera app.

5. Action Shots

Capturing fast-moving subjects, such as athletes, animals, or vehicles, can be challenging. However, the iPhone 16's camera excels in these situations with its fast shutter speeds and intelligent motion detection.

- **Burst Mode:** To capture the perfect moment, use Burst Mode by pressing and holding the shutter button. This takes a rapid series of photos, allowing you to choose the best frame. You can then scroll through the burst images and select the one with the clearest focus or most dynamic action.

- **Live Photos:** Live Photos capture a few seconds of video before and after you press the shutter, giving you the ability to choose the exact moment you want to freeze. You can activate Live Photos by tapping the Live Photo icon in the Camera app. This is great for capturing moments with subtle movements, like waves crashing or a person smiling.

Video Recording and Editing

The iPhone 16's video capabilities are among the best in the smartphone world. Whether you're capturing 4K video, shooting in slow motion, or editing your footage on the go, the iPhone 16 provides the tools needed for creating high-quality content.

1. 4K Video Recording

The iPhone 16 supports 4K video recording at up to 60 frames per second (fps), delivering cinema-quality footage in your pocket. 4K resolution provides incredible detail and sharpness, making your videos look professional, whether you're shooting a vlog, a short film, or family moments.

- **Switching to 4K:** To enable 4K recording, go to Settings > Camera > Record Video and select your preferred resolution and frame rate. While 24 fps provides a more cinematic look, 60 fps is ideal for capturing fast-paced action smoothly.

- **Stabilization:** The iPhone 16 includes optical image stabilization (OIS), which helps reduce the effects of camera shake, especially when shooting handheld. This ensures smoother footage, even in less-than-ideal conditions.

2. Slow-Motion and Time-Lapse

In addition to standard video recording, the iPhone 16 offers slow-motion and time-lapse features, which can add creative flair to your videos.

- **Slow-Motion:** The slow-motion feature allows you to capture video at 120 or 240 fps, which can be played back at a much slower speed for dramatic effect. Slow-motion is ideal for capturing fast-moving subjects in detail, such as splashing water, sports events, or dance performances. To use this feature, swipe to Slo-Mo in the Camera app.

- **Time-Lapse:** Time-lapse condenses long periods into a shorter video, making it great for capturing sunsets, cityscapes, or plant growth. The iPhone 16's time-lapse mode automatically adjusts the frame rate based on the duration of your recording, ensuring smooth and consistent playback.

3. Built-In Editing Tools

Once you've recorded your video, the iPhone 16 provides a comprehensive set of editing tools directly in the Photos app. Here's how you can enhance your footage:

- **Trimming:** You can easily trim the beginning or end of your video to remove unwanted sections. Open your video in Photos, tap Edit, and drag the handles on either end of the timeline to shorten the clip.

- **Filters and Adjustments:** Similar to photo editing, you can apply filters to your videos or adjust settings like exposure, contrast, saturation, and brightness. Tap Edit, then select the adjustment icons at the bottom of the screen to tweak these parameters.

- **Adding Music:** You can add a soundtrack to your video directly from the iMovie app. Open your video in iMovie, tap the + button, and select Audio to choose a song from your library or Apple Music.

- **Adjusting Focus in Cinematic Mode:** If you recorded your video in Cinematic Mode, you can adjust the focus points after recording. Tap Edit on your video, and use the focus sliders to select which parts of the scene should remain sharp.

The iPhone 16's camera system is a powerhouse of photographic and videographic technology, providing users with professional-grade tools in a portable device. From ProRAW and ProRes for professionals to Night Mode and Portrait Mode for casual users, there's something for everyone in this highly advanced system. Whether you're capturing photos or videos, the combination of powerful hardware and intelligent software ensures that every moment you record looks as stunning as possible.

CHAPTER 6

BATTERY MANAGEMENT AND PERFORMANCE OPTIMIZATION

*****

The iPhone 16 series offers a range of powerful features, cutting-edge technology, and a refined user experience, but all of these benefits depend on the device's performance and battery life. Properly managing your iPhone's battery health and optimizing its performance is essential for ensuring a smooth and seamless user experience. In this chapter, we'll explore best practices for maintaining battery health, tips for using Low Power Mode effectively, and methods for performance optimization that keep your iPhone running at its best.

Battery Health and Charging Tips

Battery health plays a crucial role in determining how long your iPhone can last on a single charge, and it also impacts the longevity of the battery over time. While the iPhone 16 comes equipped with advanced battery technology, it's important to follow certain guidelines to preserve the health of the battery and extend its lifespan.

1. Checking Battery Health

Apple includes a built-in Battery Health feature that allows users to monitor the condition of their battery over time. This feature shows you important metrics like Maximum Capacity and Peak Performance Capability, which indicate how well the battery is functioning.

- **To check battery health**, go to Settings > Battery > Battery Health & Charging. Here, you'll see a percentage labeled Maximum Capacity, which tells you how much capacity your battery currently holds compared to when it was new. For example, if the battery's maximum capacity is 90%, it means that the battery can hold 90% of its original charge.

- Peak Performance Capability: This section will indicate whether your battery can still support peak performance, meaning it can deliver the necessary power to handle demanding tasks without issues. If your battery health has significantly deteriorated, you may see a message indicating that the battery is no longer able to sustain peak performance.

- Optimized Battery Charging: One way to maintain battery health is to enable Optimized Battery Charging in the Battery Health settings. This feature slows down the rate at which your iPhone charges past 80% during extended charging sessions. The iPhone learns your charging habits and delays full charging until you need it, helping to reduce the wear on the battery and extend its overall lifespan.

2. Optimizing Charging

The way you charge your iPhone can have a significant impact on battery health over time. Here are some tips to help you optimize charging and extend battery life:

- **Avoid Extreme Temperatures:** Both extreme heat and cold can negatively affect your iPhone's battery health. Apple recommends keeping your iPhone between 32°F and 95°F (0°C and 35°C) for optimal performance. Charging your iPhone in extremely hot environments (such as inside a car on a sunny day) can lead to permanent damage to the battery.

- **Charge to 80%:** While it may seem counterintuitive, charging your iPhone to 100% frequently isn't necessary and can reduce battery longevity over time. If possible, aim to keep your battery between 20% and 80% for daily use. This reduces the strain on the battery and helps prevent capacity loss over time.

- **Use the Right Charger:** The iPhone 16 supports fast charging with a 20W or higher power adapter, which can charge the phone to 50% in about 30 minutes. However, using a lower-wattage charger or off-brand charging cables can lead to slower charging times and may affect battery health. For optimal results, use Apple-certified chargers and cables.

- Wireless Charging and Heat: Wireless charging is a convenient way to power up your iPhone, but it can generate more heat compared to traditional wired charging. If you frequently use wireless charging, make sure the phone is positioned correctly on the charger and placed in a well-ventilated area to prevent overheating.

3. Prolonging Battery Life

To prolong the daily battery life of your iPhone and reduce the need for frequent charging, there are several steps you can take:

- Background Activity: Many apps continue to run in the background even when you're not using them, which can drain your battery. You can manage which apps are allowed to refresh in the background by going to Settings > General > Background App Refresh and selecting Off for apps that you don't need to update in the background.

- Location Services: Certain apps use your location continuously, which can consume battery power. To save battery, go to Settings > Privacy > Location Services and review which apps have access to your location. For most apps, select While Using the App to prevent them from tracking your location unnecessarily.

- Brightness and Display: Your iPhone's display is one of the biggest battery drains. Adjust the screen brightness by swiping down from the top-right corner of the screen to access Control Center, then adjust the brightness slider. Alternatively, you can enable Auto-Brightness in Settings > Accessibility > Display & Text Size to let your iPhone adjust brightness based on ambient lighting conditions.

- Reduce Notifications: Constant notifications can cause your screen to wake up frequently, draining battery life. Go to Settings > Notifications and customize notification preferences for each app. Turning off unnecessary notifications can reduce battery consumption.

Low Power Mode

When your battery is running low and you want to extend its life until you can recharge, Low Power Mode is a useful tool. This mode temporarily reduces the iPhone's performance and limits background processes to conserve battery power.

1. When to Use Low Power Mode

Low Power Mode is designed to activate automatically when your iPhone's battery drops to 20%, but you can manually enable it at any time to prolong battery life. Low Power Mode reduces power consumption by disabling or scaling back features such as:

- **Background App Refresh:** Apps will not update content in the background, reducing power usage.

- **Email Fetch:** Your iPhone will stop fetching new emails automatically, so you'll need to refresh manually to receive new messages.

- Visual Effects: Certain visual effects, like motion and transparency, are reduced to minimize the strain on the processor and save power.

- Auto-Lock: The Auto-Lock feature is shortened to 30 seconds, ensuring that your screen isn't left on unnecessarily when you're not using the phone.

2. How to Enable Low Power Mode

To manually turn on Low Power Mode, go to Settings > Battery and toggle on Low Power Mode. You'll know it's active when the battery icon in the top-right corner of the screen turns yellow. You can also add Low Power Mode to the Control Center for quick access. To do this, go to Settings > Control Center and tap the green + icon next to Low Power Mode.

Using Low Power Mode regularly can be especially useful if you're traveling, spending the day outdoors, or in a situation where you won't have access to a charger for a while. Just keep in mind that while Low Power Mode can significantly extend battery life, it does so by reducing performance, so some apps may run more slowly or behave differently.

3. Background Activity Management

Managing background activity is one of the most effective ways to conserve battery life, especially when using Low Power Mode. Here are a few additional tips for managing background activity:

- **Limit Push Notifications:** In Settings > Notifications, disable push notifications for apps that don't need to alert you in real-time. This will reduce the amount of activity happening in the background.

- **Manage iCloud Sync:** While iCloud is great for syncing your data across devices, constant syncing can drain your battery. To reduce iCloud activity, go to Settings > [Your Name] > iCloud and toggle off iCloud sync for apps that you don't need to update continuously.

- Turn Off Background Activity for Battery-Intensive Apps: In Settings > Battery, you can see a list of apps that are using the most battery. If certain apps are consuming too much power, you can disable their background activity or limit how often you use them.

Performance Tips

Keeping your iPhone 16 running smoothly involves more than just managing battery life. Proper performance optimization through system maintenance, app management, and storage optimization can help ensure that your device stays fast and responsive over time.

1. System Maintenance

Regular system maintenance ensures that your iPhone is running at peak performance. Here are a few key steps to maintain your iPhone's performance:

- **Keep iOS Up to Date:** Apple regularly releases updates for iOS that include bug fixes, performance improvements, and security patches. Always make sure that your iPhone is running the latest version of iOS by going to Settings > General > Software Update. Automatic updates can be enabled to ensure your device stays current without manual intervention.

- Restart Your iPhone: It may seem simple, but restarting your iPhone occasionally can help refresh the system and clear temporary files or minor bugs that could be slowing down performance. To restart, press and hold the Side Button and one of the volume buttons until the power-off slider appears.

- Clear Browser Cache: Over time, Safari and other browsers store cache files that can slow down your phone. You can clear Safari's cache by going to Settings > Safari > Clear History and Website Data. This helps free up space and improve browsing speed.

2. App Management

Managing apps effectively is crucial for keeping your iPhone running efficiently. Overloaded storage or resource-hungry apps can slow down your phone and drain battery life.

- Uninstall Unused Apps: Many users accumulate apps over time that they no longer use. Go to Settings > General > iPhone Storage to see a list of apps and how much storage they're using. If an app hasn't been used in a while, consider deleting it to free up space. You can also enable Offload Unused Apps, which automatically removes apps you haven't used in a long time while keeping your documents and data intact.

- Close Background Apps: While iOS is efficient at managing background apps, closing apps you're not using can still help save resources. Swipe up from the bottom of the screen (or double-click the Home button on older iPhones) to open the App Switcher, then swipe up on apps to close them.

- Limit Resource-Intensive Apps: Certain apps, such as games, video editors, and social media platforms, are more resource-intensive than others. To maintain optimal performance, limit how frequently you use these apps, especially when running multiple apps simultaneously.

3. Storage Optimization

Running out of storage can slow down your iPhone, so keeping an eye on storage levels is essential. Here are a few ways to optimize storage on your iPhone:

- Optimize Photo Storage: Photos and videos can take up a significant amount of space on your iPhone. To optimize storage, go to Settings > Photos and select Optimize iPhone Storage. This option stores full-resolution photos and videos in iCloud while keeping smaller, lower-resolution versions on your device. When you need the full-resolution file, it will download from iCloud automatically.

- Review Downloaded Files and Media: Go through apps like Files, Messages, and WhatsApp to delete large files or media that are no longer needed. For instance, videos, voice messages, and images in messaging apps can accumulate and take up space.

- Use iCloud for Backup: Use iCloud to back up data like photos, documents, and app data. This not only helps free up local storage but also ensures that your important files are safely stored in the cloud. You can manage iCloud storage by going to Settings > [Your Name] > iCloud > Manage Storage.

- Check for Large Apps: In Settings > General > iPhone Storage, you can see which apps are consuming the most storage. Review the list and consider offloading or deleting apps that are taking up more space than necessary.

Battery management and performance optimization are crucial for getting the most out of your iPhone 16. By following best practices for battery health, effectively using Low Power Mode, and optimizing performance through system maintenance and app management, you can ensure that your iPhone remains fast, efficient, and reliable. Whether you're trying to extend battery life during a busy day or keep your device running smoothly over the long term, these tips will help you maximize the potential of your iPhone 16.

CHAPTER 7

SECURITY AND PRIVACY

*****

In today's interconnected world, security and privacy are more important than ever. With the iPhone 16, Apple continues to prioritize user privacy and data protection, offering a wide array of features designed to keep your personal information safe. From biometric authentication to location services and data tracking controls, the iPhone 16 equips users with the tools necessary to protect their devices and information. In this chapter, we'll explore the fundamentals of security and privacy on your iPhone 16, including Face ID and Passcode Security, detailed Privacy Settings, and the essential Find My iPhone feature for locating lost or stolen devices.

Face ID and Passcode Security

One of the most vital aspects of keeping your iPhone secure is controlling access to it. Apple's Face ID system and traditional Passcode Security offer powerful ways to ensure that your data is protected, even if your phone falls into the wrong hands.

1. Setting Up Face ID

Face ID is Apple's facial recognition technology, offering a seamless and secure way to unlock your iPhone, authorize purchases, and access sensitive data. The iPhone 16 features an advanced version of Face ID, which uses a TrueDepth camera system to map and recognize your facial features with incredible accuracy, even in low-light conditions or if you're wearing glasses, a hat, or a face mask.

Here's how to set up Face ID on your iPhone 16:

1. Open Settings: Navigate to Settings > Face ID & Passcode.

2. Create a Passcode: If you haven't already set up a passcode, you'll need to create one. The passcode serves as a backup method of authentication in case Face ID fails.

3. Register Your Face: Tap Set Up Face ID. Hold your iPhone in portrait orientation and position your face within the frame. You'll be prompted to move your head in a circle so the camera can capture multiple angles of your face. This ensures that Face ID can recognize you from different perspectives.

4. Complete the Scan: After the first scan is complete, you'll be asked to perform a second scan to capture additional facial data. Once both scans are done, Face ID will be ready to use.

Face ID is not only fast and convenient but also extremely secure. The probability that someone else's face could unlock your iPhone is one in a million, making it far more secure than traditional fingerprint or PIN-based systems. Additionally, Face ID data is stored locally on your device in the Secure Enclave, meaning it's never uploaded to Apple's servers or shared with third parties.

2. Maximizing Face ID Effectiveness

For the best experience with Face ID, consider the following tips:

- Enable Attention Awareness: Face ID can be set to require attention, meaning it will only unlock your iPhone if you're actively looking at it. This adds an extra layer of security by ensuring that your phone can't be unlocked if someone holds it up to your face while you're not paying attention (e.g. if you're asleep). You can enable this in Settings > Face ID & Passcode > Require Attention for Face ID.

- Use Face ID for More than Unlocking: Face ID can be used for a variety of functions beyond simply unlocking your phone. You can enable it for use with Apple Pay, app authentication, and auto-filling passwords. These options can be found under Settings > Face ID & Passcode.

- Allow Face ID with a Mask: With the iPhone 16, Face ID can recognize you even if you're wearing a mask. Go to Settings > Face ID & Passcode and enable

Face ID with a Mask to improve its accuracy when you're masked.

3. Choosing a Strong Passcode

Although Face ID is the primary method of unlocking your iPhone, having a strong Passcode is essential as a backup. If Face ID fails or if the phone hasn't been unlocked for an extended period, your iPhone will prompt you for your passcode.

Here are some best practices for setting a secure passcode:

- **Avoid Simple Passcodes:** While a four-digit passcode is convenient, it's also easier to guess. Opt for a six-digit passcode or, better yet, choose a custom alphanumeric code that includes both numbers and letters. To change your passcode, go to Settings > Face ID & Passcode > Change Passcode.

- **Disable Simple Passcode:** If you're using a four-digit passcode, consider upgrading to a longer one. You can switch to a six-digit passcode or custom code by selecting Passcode Options when setting or changing your passcode.

- Lock Screen Security: You can also manage what information is accessible from the Lock Screen by going to Settings > Face ID & Passcode and scrolling down to the Allow Access When Locked section. From here, you can control whether things like Today View, Notification Center, and Siri can be accessed without unlocking the phone. Limiting what's visible on the Lock Screen adds a layer of protection.

Privacy Settings

Apple's dedication to user privacy is a cornerstone of its iOS ecosystem, and the iPhone 16 comes equipped with several privacy-enhancing features. By configuring these settings, you can control which apps have access to your data, manage location sharing, and block unnecessary tracking.

1. App Tracking Transparency

One of the most important privacy features in iOS is App Tracking Transparency (ATT). ATT allows you to control whether apps are permitted to track your activity across other websites and apps for advertising purposes. By default, apps are required to ask for your permission before tracking your data.

To manage App Tracking Transparency:

1. Go to Settings > Privacy & Security > Tracking.

2. You'll see a list of apps that have requested tracking permission. You can toggle tracking on or off for each app individually.

3. For maximum privacy, you can toggle off Allow Apps to Request to Track, which prevents any app from even asking to track you in the future.

By limiting tracking, you can reduce the amount of data that advertisers collect about your online behavior. This won't impact your ability to use the apps, but it will stop them from showing you targeted ads based on your activity across other apps and websites.

2. Managing Location Permissions

Location services are used by many apps for navigation, recommendations, and even social features. However, you have control over which apps can access your location and when they can do so.

To manage location permissions:

1. Go to Settings > Privacy & Security > Location Services.

2. You'll see a list of apps with their current location access settings. Tap on an app to adjust its permissions. *The options include:*

- **Never:** The app cannot access your location.

- **Ask Next Time:** The app will ask for permission to use your location the next time it needs it.

- **While Using the App:** The app can only access your location when it's open and actively in use.

- **Always:** The app can access your location at any time, even when it's running in the background.

For most apps, Using the App is the best option, as it ensures that the app can only track your location when necessary. Always review your location settings periodically to ensure apps aren't accessing your location unnecessarily.

3. Apple's Built-In Privacy Features

Apple has introduced several built-in privacy features in iOS 17 that give you more control over your personal information:

- Mail Privacy Protection: This feature prevents email senders from tracking your location or whether you've opened their messages. To enable it, go to Settings > Mail > Privacy Protection. This is particularly useful for avoiding marketing emails that use invisible tracking pixels to gather data about your interactions.

- Private Relay: For users with an iCloud+ subscription, Private Relay is a feature that encrypts your internet traffic, ensuring that websites and advertisers can't track your browsing activity. It works by hiding your IP address and location, adding an extra layer of anonymity when using Safari. Private Relay can be enabled in Settings > [Your Name] > iCloud > Private Relay.

- Hide My Email: Another iCloud+ feature, Hide My Email allows you to create random email addresses that forward to your real inbox. This way, you can sign up for online services or newsletters without revealing your actual email address. You can manage or create new addresses by going to Settings > [Your Name] > iCloud > Hide My Email.

- App Privacy Reports: In Settings > Privacy & Security > App Privacy Report, you can access detailed information about how apps are using your data. The report shows how often apps access your camera, microphone, location, and other sensitive data, giving you the insight needed to adjust permissions as necessary.

Find My iPhone

One of the most useful security tools on your iPhone is the Find My iPhone feature. Whether your device is misplaced or stolen, Find My allows you to locate it, secure it, and even erase it remotely. Here's how you can make the most of this powerful feature.

1. Setting Up Find My iPhone

If you haven't already, make sure Find My iPhone is enabled:

1. Open Settings and tap your name at the top to access your Apple ID settings.

2. Select Find My.

3. Tap Find My iPhone and toggle it on.

Make sure that Find My Network is also enabled. This feature allows your iPhone to be located even if it's offline by using a network of nearby Apple devices.

2. Locating Your Device

If your iPhone is lost, you can use another device or a web browser to locate it:

1. Open the Find My app on another Apple device, or visit iCloud.com on any browser and log in with your Apple ID.

2. Select Find iPhone to see the last known location of your device. If the iPhone is online, it will show its current location on the map.

3. From here, you can use several options:

- **Play Sound:** This will trigger a loud sound on your iPhone, making it easier to find if it's nearby.

- **Directions:** Tap this option to get step-by-step directions to your iPhone's location.

- **Notify When Found:** If your iPhone is offline, this option will notify you when it reconnects to the network.

3. Sharing Locations

Find My also allows you to share your location with friends and family. To share your location:

1. Open the Find My app and go to the People tab.

2. Tap Start Sharing Location and choose the contact you want to share your location with.

3. You can choose to share your location Indefinitely, Until the End of the Day, or for a Specific Time.

Sharing your location with family or close friends can be useful for coordinating meetups or providing peace of mind when traveling.

4. Activating Lost Mode

If your iPhone is lost or stolen, you can activate Lost Mode to lock it remotely and display a custom message with your contact information. Lost Mode also prevents anyone from turning off Find My or resetting the device without your Apple ID.

To activate Lost Mode:

1. Open the Find My app or visit iCloud.com.

2. Select your iPhone and tap Mark As Lost.

3. Enter a phone number where you can be reached and a message to display on the iPhone's Lock Screen.

When Lost Mode is enabled, your iPhone will be locked, and you'll receive location updates when the device moves. If you recover your device, you can easily turn off Lost Mode by entering your passcode.

5. Erasing Your iPhone Remotely

If your iPhone contains sensitive data and you fear it's been stolen, you can remotely erase all the data on the device. This should only be done as a last resort, as it will prevent you from tracking the iPhone further.

To erase your iPhone:

1. Open the Find My app or visit iCloud.com.

2. Select your iPhone and choose Erase iPhone.

3. Confirm the action and all of your data will be wiped from the device.

Keep in mind that this action is permanent. After erasing your iPhone, you can no longer use Find My to locate it.

Security and privacy are paramount in today's digital landscape, and Apple's iPhone 16 offers a comprehensive suite of features to protect your personal information. From Face ID and strong Passcode Security to App Tracking Transparency and Find My iPhone, you have the tools necessary to safeguard your device and data. By following the tips and best practices outlined in this chapter, you can ensure that your iPhone remains secure, your privacy is maintained, and your information stays in your control.

CHAPTER 8

ICLOUD AND BACKUP

*****

The iPhone 16 offers an extensive array of features, but none are more essential for data protection and seamless device synchronization than iCloud. With iCloud, Apple ensures that your data is automatically backed up and accessible across your devices, whether it's photos, documents, or app data. In this chapter, we will explore iCloud's full range of capabilities, dive into backup options that help you secure your device data, and discuss storage management to help you effectively organize your files while preventing clutter. Understanding how to properly use iCloud and manage your backups ensures your information is protected and readily available whenever you need it.

Using iCloud

iCloud is Apple's cloud-based storage and syncing service that seamlessly integrates with all your Apple devices. Whether you're using an iPhone, iPad, Mac, or Apple Watch, iCloud ensures that your files, photos, and data stay updated across all devices in real time. Beyond just file storage, iCloud provides key features such as iCloud Photos, iCloud Drive, and device backups that make it an essential service for every iPhone user.

1. iCloud Photos

One of the most popular features of iCloud is iCloud Photos, which automatically stores your entire photo library in the cloud. This not only ensures that your photos are backed up in case of a lost or damaged device but also allows you to access your photos from any Apple device signed into your iCloud account.

Benefits of iCloud Photos:

- **Seamless Synchronization:** All photos and videos you take on your iPhone are instantly uploaded to iCloud and available across your other devices, including your Mac, iPad, and Apple TV.

- **Optimized Storage:** iCloud Photos includes an Optimize iPhone Storage option that helps free up space on your device. When this is enabled, full-resolution photos and videos are stored in iCloud, while smaller, lower-resolution versions remain on your iPhone. This way, you can keep thousands of photos on your device without worrying about running out of space.

- **Shared Albums:** iCloud makes it easy to share photo albums with friends and family. You can create shared albums that allow others to view, comment, and even add their photos to the collection.

To enable iCloud Photos:

1. Go to Settings > [Your Name] > iCloud.

2. Select Photos and toggle on iCloud Photos.

3. For optimized storage, choose Optimize iPhone Storage.

With iCloud Photos, you don't have to worry about losing your memories if something happens to your device. Every image and video is automatically backed up and accessible across all your Apple devices and via iCloud.com.

2. iCloud Drive

While iCloud Photos handles your multimedia files, iCloud Drive manages documents, app data, and files from other sources, offering a flexible, cloud-based file storage system.

Key Features of iCloud Drive:

- **File Synchronization:** iCloud Drive keeps your files synchronized across all devices. Whether you're working on a Pages document on your Mac or accessing it from your iPhone, your files remain consistent across all devices.

- Folder Sharing: You can share entire folders with other iCloud users. This is ideal for collaborative projects, where multiple people need access to the same documents.

- App Integration: Many iPhone apps integrate with iCloud Drive to store data and documents directly in the cloud. Apps like Pages, Numbers, and Keynote automatically save files to iCloud Drive so you can access them from any device.

To enable iCloud Drive:

1. Go to Settings > [Your Name] > iCloud > iCloud Drive and toggle it on.

2. You can also manage individual app settings to decide which apps store their data in iCloud Drive.

iCloud Drive provides a convenient way to store and organize all types of files, ensuring that they're accessible from anywhere, anytime.

3. Device Backups

Perhaps one of the most critical features of iCloud is its ability to perform automatic device backups. Backing up your iPhone regularly is essential to protect your data in case your device is lost, damaged, or replaced. With iCloud, your iPhone is automatically backed up every time it is connected to Wi-Fi and charging, meaning you'll always have a recent backup available.

What is Backed Up in iCloud?

- **App Data:** iCloud backs up data from your installed apps, including app settings, progress in games, and configuration files.

- **Messages and Contacts:** iCloud ensures that all your text messages, iMessages, and contacts are saved.

- **Device Settings:** iCloud stores important settings such as Wi-Fi passwords, wallpaper choices, and Home Screen layouts.

- Health Data: If you're using Apple Health, all of your health-related information, such as step counts and activity levels, is backed up securely in iCloud.

To enable iCloud Backup:

1. Go to Settings > [Your Name] > iCloud > iCloud Backup.

2. Toggle on iCloud Backup. Your iPhone will now automatically back up to iCloud when connected to Wi-Fi and charging.

iCloud Backups are a lifesaver in case you ever need to restore your iPhone or set up a new iPhone with all your previous data intact.

Backup Options

While iCloud provides an effortless way to back up your iPhone automatically, some users may prefer to manually manage their backups. In addition to iCloud backups, Apple offers manual backup options via iTunes or Finder on your Mac or PC, allowing for more flexibility and control over the backup process.

1. iCloud Backup

The simplest and most hands-off method is to use iCloud Backup. As mentioned earlier, iCloud performs automatic backups in the background whenever your iPhone is charging and connected to Wi-Fi.

How to Initiate a Manual iCloud Backup:

1. Go to Settings > [Your Name] > iCloud > iCloud Backup.

2. Tap Back Up Now to create an immediate backup of your iPhone.

iCloud Backup is ideal for users who prefer a seamless and automatic solution, but it does require sufficient iCloud storage space, which may necessitate upgrading your iCloud storage plan.

2. Manual Backup via Finder (Mac) or iTunes (Windows)

For users who prefer to keep their backups offline or want greater control over the backup process, manual backups via Finder on Mac or iTunes on Windows provide an excellent alternative. Manual backups can also store more data than iCloud, such as downloaded media and app files, and can be saved to your computer's local storage.

How to Back Up Using Finder (on Mac):

1. Connect your iPhone to your Mac using a USB cable.

2. Open Finder and select your iPhone from the sidebar under Locations.

3. In the General tab, select Back Up All of the Data on Your iPhone to This Mac.

4. If you want to encrypt your backup, check Encrypt Local Backup and create a password.

5. Click Back Up Now to start the backup process.

How to Back Up Using iTunes (on Windows):

1. Connect your iPhone to your PC using a USB cable.

2. Open iTunes and select your iPhone from the top-left corner.

3. In the Summary tab, under Backups, select This Computer.

4. If you wish to encrypt your backup, check Encrypt iPhone Backup and create a password.

5. Click Back Up Now to begin the process.

Manual backups are a great option for users who want more control over where their data is stored, and they don't require internet access like iCloud backups.

3. Restoring from Backup

Whether you're switching to a new device or restoring your current iPhone, restoring from a backup is a straightforward process. With both iCloud and manual backups, you can seamlessly restore all your apps, settings, and data onto your iPhone.

To restore from an iCloud Backup:

1. When setting up a new iPhone or resetting your current iPhone, choose Restore from iCloud Backup during the setup process.

2. Sign in with your Apple ID and select the backup you want to restore from.

To restore from a Finder or iTunes Backup:

1. Connect your iPhone to your Mac or PC using a USB cable.

2. Open Finder (on Mac) or iTunes (on Windows).

3. Select your iPhone and choose Restore Backup.

4. Select the backup you want to restore from and click Restore.

Restoring from a backup ensures that all of your photos, contacts, apps, and settings are transferred to your new or reset device, making the transition seamless.

Storage Management

iCloud offers up to 5 GB of free storage, but as you accumulate photos, apps, and backups, you may quickly find yourself running out of space. Managing your iCloud storage effectively allows you to keep important data backed up while freeing up unnecessary files that may be taking up valuable space.

1. Checking iCloud Storage

To check how much storage you're using in iCloud:

1. Go to Settings > [Your Name] > iCloud.

2. Tap Manage Storage to view a breakdown of what's taking up space, including photos, backups, documents, and apps.

You can see how much storage each category is using, making it easier to decide what to delete or manage.

2. Managing iCloud Backups

One of the most common reasons for iCloud storage filling up is old or unnecessary backups. If you have multiple devices connected to the same Apple ID, you may have backups for each one taking up space.

To manage and delete old backups:

1. Go to Settings > [Your Name] > iCloud > Manage Storage > Backups.

2. Select the device backup you want to delete and tap Delete Backup.

If you're no longer using a device, deleting its backup can free up a significant amount of iCloud space.

3. Optimizing iCloud Photos

If you have iCloud Photos enabled, your photos and videos may be using a large portion of your iCloud storage. While iCloud offers the Optimize iPhone

Storage option to reduce local storage usage, the full-resolution versions of your photos remain in iCloud.

To manage iCloud Photos:

1. Go to Settings > [Your Name] > iCloud > Photos.

2. Select Optimize iPhone Storage to store smaller versions of your photos on your device while keeping the full-resolution originals in iCloud.

You can also manage specific albums or delete unwanted photos directly from the Photos app to free up additional space.

4. Upgrading iCloud Storage

If you find that managing storage isn't enough and you consistently run out of space, upgrading to a paid iCloud plan may be necessary. Apple offers several iCloud+ plans to expand your storage capacity beyond the free 5 GB limit.

iCloud+ plans:

- 50 GB Plan: Ideal for light users who need a bit more space for photos and app data.

- 200 GB Plan: Perfect for users with multiple devices or larger photo libraries.

- 2 TB Plan: Best for families or users who rely heavily on iCloud for backups, files, and photo storage.

To upgrade your iCloud storage:

1. Go to Settings > [Your Name] > iCloud > Manage Storage.

2. Select Change Storage Plan and choose your preferred option.

Upgrading your iCloud storage ensures that you always have enough space for photos, documents, and backups, providing peace of mind that your data is safely stored and accessible.

iCloud is a vital tool for any iPhone 16 user, offering seamless synchronization, storage, and backup capabilities across all your Apple devices. Whether you're backing up essential files, sharing photos, or ensuring your iPhone is protected with automatic backups, iCloud helps keep your data safe, accessible and organized. Understanding how to manage your storage, use manual backups, and optimize iCloud for your needs ensures that you get the most out of your iPhone 16 and maintain control over your valuable information. With the tips and best practices covered in this chapter, you can confidently use iCloud and backup options to safeguard your data and enjoy a hassle-free experience.

CHAPTER 9

CONNECTIVITY AND ACCESSORIES

*****

The iPhone 16 offers a seamless experience when it comes to connectivity and compatibility with a range of accessories. Whether you're transferring files, managing wireless connections, or enhancing your iPhone experience with Apple accessories like AirPods and Apple Watch, the iPhone 16 ensures fast, easy, and intuitive connectivity options. In this chapter, we'll dive deep into Bluetooth and AirDrop, explain how to optimize your Wi-Fi and cellular settings and provide guidance on using AirPods, Apple Watch, and other accessories to get the most out of your device.

Bluetooth and AirDrop

Bluetooth and AirDrop are two of the most efficient ways to wirelessly connect devices and transfer files between Apple products. The iPhone 16 makes these features even more user-friendly and accessible, whether you're syncing Bluetooth headphones or sharing documents with nearby iPhones or Macs.

1. Connecting to Bluetooth Devices

Bluetooth allows your iPhone 16 to wirelessly connect to a variety of devices, including headphones, speakers, keyboards, mice, smart home devices, and fitness trackers. Bluetooth's low energy consumption ensures that your iPhone's battery isn't drained quickly during these connections, making it a reliable tool for frequent wireless interaction.

How to Connect to Bluetooth Devices:

1. Go to Settings > Bluetooth and toggle Bluetooth on.

2. *Your iPhone will automatically start scanning for nearby Bluetooth devices. Make sure the device you want to connect to is in pairing mode.*

3. *Tap the name of the device when it appears on the screen to pair.*

4. *Depending on the device, you may be asked to enter a passcode (e.g., for Bluetooth keyboards), which is usually provided in the device's manual.*

Once paired, your iPhone will remember the device for future use. Bluetooth devices will automatically reconnect when they are within range and turned on.

Troubleshooting Bluetooth Connections:

- **Device Not Appearing:** If the device you're trying to connect to doesn't appear, make sure it's in pairing mode, and check if the Bluetooth device is charged or turned on.

- **Connection Issues:** If you're having trouble connecting, try turning off and on both your iPhone's

Bluetooth and the Bluetooth device, or restart your iPhone.

- **Removing Devices:** If you no longer use a Bluetooth device, go to Settings > Bluetooth, tap the i icon next to the device, and select Forget This Device to remove it from your list of paired devices.

2. Transferring Files via AirDrop

AirDrop is a fast, wireless file-sharing feature exclusive to Apple devices. It uses both Bluetooth and Wi-Fi technology to transfer files, photos, videos, documents, and even website links between iPhones, iPads, and Macs. The key advantage of AirDrop is that it does not require an internet connection—only proximity and enabled Bluetooth and Wi-Fi features on both devices.

How to Use AirDrop:

1. Ensure Bluetooth and Wi-Fi are enabled on both the sending and receiving devices. AirDrop does not require a Wi-Fi network, but both devices must have Wi-Fi turned on.

2. Open the file, photo, or item you want to share.

3. Tap the Share icon (a box with an arrow pointing up) and select AirDrop.

4. Choose the recipient from the list of nearby Apple devices.

5. The recipient will receive a notification and must accept the AirDrop file transfer for it to proceed.

To ensure privacy and avoid unwanted file-sharing, you can control who can send you files via AirDrop:

1. Go to Settings > General > AirDrop and select:

  - Receiving Off: No one can send you files.

  - Contacts Only: Only your contacts can AirDrop files to you.

  - Everyone: Anyone nearby with an Apple device can send files.

AirDrop Troubleshooting:

- **Devices Not Appearing:** Ensure both Bluetooth and Wi-Fi are enabled on both devices and make sure AirDrop is set to Everyone or Contacts Only. Additionally, the devices need to be within approximately 30 feet (9 meters) of each other.

- **AirDrop Not Sending:** If you're having trouble, restart both devices or toggle AirDrop on and off in the Control Center. In some cases, disabling Personal Hotspot in Settings > Cellular can help resolve issues.

Wi-Fi and Cellular Settings

The iPhone 16 is designed to effortlessly transition between Wi-Fi and cellular networks, allowing you to stay connected wherever you go. Understanding how to manage your data, set up eSIMs, and use features like Wi-Fi Calling can optimize your network experience and help save on data usage.

1. Managing Wi-Fi Settings

Wi-Fi is an essential component for fast internet browsing, app downloads, and media streaming without consuming cellular data. On the iPhone 16, managing Wi-Fi connections is quick and intuitive.

How to Connect to a Wi-Fi Network:

1. Go to Settings > Wi-Fi and toggle Wi-Fi on.

2. Your iPhone will display a list of available networks. Select your preferred network from the list.

3. If prompted, enter the network password and tap Join.

Once connected, your iPhone will automatically reconnect to this network whenever you're in range, reducing the need to repeatedly enter passwords.

Advanced Wi-Fi Settings:

- **Auto-Join:** To prevent your iPhone from automatically joining certain networks, go to Settings > Wi-Fi, tap the i icon next to the network, and toggle Auto-Join off. This is useful for avoiding slow or unsecured public networks.

- **Private Wi-Fi Address:** In iOS 17, Apple introduced Private Wi-Fi Addresses to protect your privacy. Each Wi-Fi network you join will assign a unique MAC address to your iPhone, preventing network operators from tracking your activity across different networks. This is enabled by default, but you can turn it off for specific networks if needed in Settings > Wi-Fi > [Network Name] > Private Address.

2. Managing Cellular Data and eSIM

When you're not connected to Wi-Fi, your iPhone 16 uses a cellular data connection to access the internet. Understanding your data plan and controlling your cellular usage can help prevent overage fees and optimize your network experience.

Monitoring Cellular Data Usage:

To view and manage your cellular data usage:

1. Go to Settings > Cellular (or Mobile Data).

2. Under Cellular Data Usage, you can see your total data usage for the current period. Scroll down to see how much data individual apps have consumed.

Managing Data Settings:

- **Enable/Disable Cellular Data:** If you want to limit data usage, especially when nearing your data limit, you can toggle Cellular Data off at the top of the Cellular settings screen.

- Low Data Mode: Enable Low Data Mode in Settings > Cellular > Cellular Data Options to reduce your data usage. This mode pauses background app activity, automatic downloads, and visual effects that consume data.

- Wi-Fi Assist: This feature, found in Settings > Cellular, automatically switches to cellular data if your Wi-Fi connection is poor. While it's useful for maintaining a stable connection, turning it off can help conserve data usage.

Setting Up eSIM and Dual SIM

The iPhone 16 supports eSIM, a digital SIM card that replaces the need for a physical SIM card. This allows you to use two different phone numbers or carriers simultaneously, making the iPhone 16 a great option for frequent travelers or those who need separate lines for work and personal use.

How to Set Up an eSIM:

1. Go to Settings > Cellular and tap Add Cellular Plan.

2. You can scan the QR code provided by your carrier or manually enter the details to activate the eSIM.

3. Once activated, you'll see the option to set your Primary and Secondary numbers, as well as configure settings for which number to use for data, voice, and messaging.

Using Dual SIM:

With Dual SIM, you can have two active phone lines on your iPhone 16. This is ideal for managing work and personal contacts separately or using local carriers when traveling abroad.

- To switch between SIMs for calls or data, go to Settings > Cellular, then choose which line you want to use as your default.

- *You can assign specific contacts to a particular SIM by editing their details in Contacts, ensuring that calls and messages go through the appropriate line.*

3. Wi-Fi Calling

Wi-Fi Calling allows you to make phone calls using your Wi-Fi network instead of your cellular connection. This is especially useful in areas with poor cellular coverage but strong Wi-Fi signals, such as in certain buildings or rural locations.

How to Enable Wi-Fi Calling:

1. Go to Settings > Cellular > Wi-Fi Calling.

2. Toggle on Wi-Fi Calling on This iPhone.

3. Follow the on-screen instructions to complete the setup, which may include entering your emergency address for 911 services.

Once enabled, your iPhone will automatically use Wi-Fi to make calls when connected to a Wi-Fi network, improving call quality and saving cellular data.

Using AirPods, Apple Watch, and Other Accessories

Apple's ecosystem of accessories, including AirPods, Apple Watch, and other third-party accessories, integrates seamlessly with the iPhone 16, enhancing both productivity and convenience. Whether you're using wireless headphones, smartwatches, or other peripherals, the iPhone 16 ensures quick and reliable pairing.

1. Using AirPods

AirPods offer a wireless, hassle-free way to enjoy music, take calls, and interact with Siri. The iPhone 16 automatically detects AirPods when they are nearby, streamlining the pairing process.

How to Pair AirPods:

1. Open the AirPods case and hold it near your iPhone.

2. A pop-up will appear on your screen. Tap Connect to pair your AirPods.

3. Once paired, your AirPods will automatically connect to your iPhone and any other Apple devices linked to your iCloud account.

Customizing AirPods Settings:

- Go to Settings > Bluetooth and tap the i icon next to your AirPods to customize settings such as Noise Control, Automatic Ear Detection, and double-tap actions for playing, pausing, or skipping tracks.

- Spatial Audio: The iPhone 16 supports Spatial Audio for a more immersive sound experience with AirPods Pro and AirPods Max. You can enable this feature in the AirPods settings to enjoy 3D audio when listening to compatible media.

2. Using Apple Watch

The Apple Watch is another essential accessory that enhances the iPhone experience, offering fitness tracking, notifications, and other health monitoring features right on your wrist. With seamless integration, you can receive calls, texts, and app notifications without taking your iPhone out of your pocket.

Pairing Apple Watch with iPhone:

1. Turn on your Apple Watch and bring it near your iPhone.

2. A prompt will appear on your iPhone screen. Tap Continue to start pairing.

3. Follow the on-screen instructions to complete the pairing process, including setting up cellular service if applicable.

Once paired, you can customize notifications, apps, and watch faces directly from the Apple Watch app on your iPhone.

3. Using Other Accessories

The iPhone 16 is compatible with a wide range of accessories, from Bluetooth speakers to gaming controllers and smart home devices. Here's a brief guide on how to pair and use other popular accessories:

Bluetooth Speakers:

1. Ensure the speaker is in pairing mode, then go to Settings > Bluetooth on your iPhone.

2. Select the speaker from the list of devices to connect.

Gaming Controllers:

The iPhone 16 supports gaming controllers such as Xbox and PlayStation controllers, which can enhance your mobile gaming experience.

1. Turn on pairing mode on the controller.

2. Go to Settings > Bluetooth and tap on the controller name to connect.

Smart Home Devices:

The iPhone 16 supports HomeKit-enabled devices, allowing you to control smart lights, locks, cameras, and more directly from the Home app.

1. Open the Home app and tap + to add a new accessory.

2. Follow the instructions to pair and configure your smart home device.

The iPhone 16 offers unparalleled connectivity and compatibility with a vast array of accessories, providing users with the flexibility to expand their device's capabilities. From wirelessly transferring files via AirDrop, managing Wi-Fi and cellular connections, to seamlessly pairing with AirPods, Apple Watch, and other accessories, the iPhone 16 allows users to stay connected and enjoy a tailored experience across multiple platforms. By mastering the connectivity and accessory features of your iPhone 16, you can elevate your daily use and enjoy a more integrated Apple ecosystem.

CHAPTER 10

APP STORE AND APPS

*****

The iPhone 16 offers users access to an incredibly vast ecosystem of apps through the App Store, along with a robust suite of native Apple apps designed to enhance productivity, creativity, and everyday life. Whether you're looking to download a new app, organize your Home Screen, or maximize the potential of Apple's pre-installed apps, mastering the App Store and its apps is essential for making the most of your iPhone 16 experience. In this chapter, we will cover how to download, update, and manage apps, provide an in-depth guide on using Apple's native apps, and offer a curated list of must-have apps for various needs, including productivity, creativity, fitness, and entertainment.

Downloading and Managing Apps

The App Store is your gateway to millions of apps, ranging from games and entertainment to productivity tools and education resources. The process of downloading, updating, and managing apps is simple, but with so many options, it's essential to know how to organize your apps efficiently.

1. Downloading Apps from the App Store

Downloading apps on the iPhone 16 is quick and easy through the App Store, where you can browse or search for apps across various categories.

Steps to Download an App:

1. Open the App Store: Tap the App Store icon on your Home Screen.

2. Search for an App: Use the search bar at the bottom right to type in the app's name or browse through categories like Top Free, Top Paid, Productivity, Games, or Health & Fitness.

3. Download the App: Once you've found the app you want, tap the Get button (for free apps) or the price (for paid apps). You may need to authenticate the download using Face ID, Touch ID, or your Apple ID password.

4. Wait for the App to Install: After the download completes, the app will appear on your Home Screen, and you can tap it to open.

In-App Purchases:

Some apps are free to download but may offer in-app purchases for additional features, content, or subscriptions. These are indicated under the app name in the App Store. Be mindful of these purchases, as they can add up over time.

2. Updating Apps

Keeping your apps updated ensures that you have access to the latest features, bug fixes, and security enhancements. You can update apps manually or enable automatic updates.

How to Manually Update Apps:

1. Open the App Store.

2. Tap your profile picture in the top-right corner of the screen.

3. Scroll down to see a list of available updates.

4. Tap Update next to an app to update it individually, or tap Update All to install all available updates at once.

Enabling Automatic Updates:

To save time, you can set your iPhone 16 to automatically update apps whenever updates are available.

1. Go to Settings > App Store.

2. Toggle on App Updates under the Automatic Downloads section.

With automatic updates enabled, your apps will update in the background without any intervention required, keeping them up to date and functioning smoothly.

3. Organizing and Managing Apps

As you download more apps, it's easy for your Home Screen to become cluttered. Organizing your apps into folders, using App Library, and customizing your layout can make navigating your iPhone more efficient.

Creating Folders:

Folders allow you to group similar apps, helping you keep your Home Screen organized.

1. Tap and hold any app icon until the icons start to jiggle.

2. Drag one app icon on top of another to create a folder.

3. The folder will automatically be named based on the app types (e.g., Social, Entertainment), but you can tap the name to edit it.

4. Drag additional apps into the folder to further organize.

Using the App Library:

The App Library is a feature introduced in iOS 14 that automatically organizes your apps into categorized folders. You can access the App Library by swiping to the right on your Home Screen.

- In the App Library, apps are sorted into categories such as Suggestions, Recently Added, and Utilities.

- You can also use the search bar at the top of the App Library to quickly find any app installed on your iPhone.

Removing Unwanted Apps:

If you no longer need an app, you can remove it to free up storage.

1. Tap and hold the app icon until a menu appears.

2. Tap Remove App, then select either Delete App to completely uninstall it or Remove from Home Screen to keep the app in the App Library but remove it from your Home Screen.

Using Apple's Native Apps

Apple's native apps are designed to work seamlessly with the iPhone's hardware and software, providing essential tools for productivity, communication, health, and navigation. While many users might be familiar with apps like Safari or Mail, the true power of Apple's native apps lies in their deeper functionality and integration across the Apple ecosystem.

1. Safari

Safari is Apple's web browser, offering fast, secure browsing with features designed to protect your privacy.

Key Features:

- **Private Browsing:** Use Private Browsing Mode to browse the web without saving your history, cookies, or form data.

- **Tab Groups:** Safari on iOS 17 introduces Tab Groups, which allow you to organize related tabs and switch between groups for different tasks (e.g., one group for work and another for personal browsing).

- Reader Mode: This feature removes ads and other distractions from web pages, providing a cleaner reading experience. Tap the Reader icon (lines at the top-left corner) when viewing an article.

Safari syncs your bookmarks, and saved passwords, and opens tabs across all your Apple devices via iCloud, ensuring a seamless browsing experience.

2. Mail

The Mail app on the iPhone 16 integrates multiple email accounts (such as iCloud, Gmail, and Outlook) into one unified inbox, making it easy to manage all your correspondence.

Key Features:

- Unified Inbox: View all your emails in a single inbox or switch between different accounts.

- Swipe Gestures: Swipe left or right on an email to quickly archive, delete, or flag it for follow-up.

- VIP Contacts: Add important contacts to your VIP list so their emails are highlighted and easily accessible.

- Search Improvements: iOS 17 introduces enhanced email search capabilities, making it easier to find messages by keywords, contacts, or subjects.

3. Maps

Apple's Maps app has evolved significantly, providing detailed maps, turn-by-turn navigation, and real-time traffic updates.

Key Features:

- Turn-by-Turn Directions: Whether you're driving, walking, or cycling, Maps provides step-by-step directions with real-time traffic conditions.

- **Look Around:** Similar to Google Street View, Look Around offers a 360-degree view of certain areas, making it easier to explore places before you visit.

- **Transit Info:** Get detailed public transportation information, including bus and train schedules, in many cities around the world.

- **Favorites:** Save frequently visited places (like home or work) to your Favorites for easy access in Maps.

Maps also integrates seamlessly with CarPlay, allowing you to view navigation directions on your car's display.

4. Notes

Notes is a versatile app for jotting down quick thoughts, creating checklists, and even collaborating with others.

Key Features:

- **Text Formatting:** Create bulleted lists, and checklists, and use rich text formatting (bold, italics, headings) to organize your notes.

- **Attachments:** Add photos, documents, or drawings to your notes, making them more dynamic and useful for brainstorming.

- **Collaboration:** Share notes with others and collaborate in real-time. Everyone you share the note with can add or edit content.

- **Folders and Tags:** Organize your notes into folders and add tags for easy categorization and search.

With iCloud sync, your notes are always up to date across all your Apple devices, allowing you to access and edit them from your iPhone, iPad, or Mac.

5. Health

The Health app is a central hub for tracking your fitness and wellness data. It pulls in information from your Apple Watch, fitness apps, and other health devices to provide a comprehensive overview of your health.

Key Features:

- **Activity Tracking:** If you use an Apple Watch, the Health app records your daily steps, distance, and calories burned, as well as data from workouts and fitness apps.

- **Health Records:** Connect your iPhone to healthcare providers to access your medical records, lab results, and immunizations.

- **Sleep Tracking:** If you wear your Apple Watch to bed, Health tracks your sleep patterns and provides insights into your sleep quality.

- **Mindfulness:** Track mindfulness sessions, such as meditation or breathing exercises, and monitor your mental well-being.

The Health app is highly customizable, allowing you to prioritize the metrics that are most important to your fitness and health goals.

App Recommendations

The App Store offers an overwhelming variety of apps, but to help you get started, here's a curated list of must-have apps that cover productivity, creativity, fitness, and entertainment. These apps can help you maximize the potential of your iPhone 16, regardless of your needs and interests.

1. Productivity Apps

1. Notion: A powerful app for note-taking, project management, and collaboration. Notion allows you to organize your work and personal life with customizable dashboards, templates, and task management tools.

2. Todoist: A leading task management app that helps you stay organized and on top of your daily to-dos. Create tasks, set reminders, and track your progress with ease.

3. Microsoft Office: Get access to Microsoft Word, Excel, and PowerPoint on your iPhone, allowing you to work on documents, spreadsheets, and presentations from anywhere.

4. Google Drive: Store and share files with Google Drive, which provides 15 GB of free cloud storage and seamless integration with Google Docs, Sheets, and Slides.

2. Creativity Apps

1. Procreate Pocket: A powerful drawing and illustration app for creatives, Procreate Pocket allows you to sketch, paint, and create digital art using a variety of tools and brushes.

2. Canva: Canva is a user-friendly design app that lets you create stunning graphics, social media posts, presentations, and more using ready-made templates.

3. Adobe Lightroom: Perfect for photographers, Lightroom provides professional-grade photo editing tools, including exposure adjustments, filters, and presets.

4. iMovie: Apple's free video editing app allows you to create movies with transitions, music, and effects, perfect for editing home videos or professional content on the go.

3. Fitness Apps

1. MyFitnessPal: Track your meals, exercise, and daily calorie intake with this comprehensive fitness app. MyFitnessPal integrates with Apple Health to monitor your overall progress.

2. Nike Training Club: Offering guided workouts ranging from strength training to yoga, Nike Training Club provides a variety of workout routines tailored to your fitness goals.

3. Headspace: A leading meditation and mindfulness app, Headspace helps you reduce stress, improve focus, and enhance your overall well-being with guided meditation sessions.

4. Strava: If you're a runner or cyclist, Strava is a must-have app for tracking your workouts, competing with friends, and analyzing your performance over time.

4. Entertainment Apps

1. Netflix: Stream your favorite TV shows, movies, and documentaries on the go with the Netflix app, offering a vast library of content.

2. Spotify: Listen to music, podcasts, and playlists with Spotify, the world's most popular streaming platform. You can create custom playlists and discover new artists tailored to your preferences.

3. Twitch: For gamers and fans of live streaming, Twitch allows you to watch your favorite streamers play games, chat with followers, and participate in live events.

4. Audible: Audible provides access to a vast collection of audiobooks across all genres. Perfect for listening to books while on the go or during your downtime.

The App Store offers endless possibilities for customizing and enhancing your iPhone 16 experience, from managing productivity to indulging in creativity, fitness, and entertainment. With Apple's robust suite of native apps and a wealth of third-party offerings, you can tailor your device to meet your specific needs and preferences. By learning how to effectively download, update, and organize apps, and taking full advantage of Apple's built-in apps, you can unlock the full potential of your iPhone 16, making it a true powerhouse for both work and play.

CHAPTER 11

APPLE SERVICES

*****

Apple's ecosystem is more than just hardware—its suite of services enhances your everyday experience with the iPhone 16. From making contactless payments with Apple Pay to enjoying on-demand entertainment with Apple Music, Apple TV+, Arcade, and Fitness+, Apple's services are designed to integrate seamlessly with your device. For users who prioritize privacy and security, iCloud+ offers advanced features like Private Relay and Hide My Email. In this chapter, we will guide you through setting up and using these services effectively, so you can take full advantage of what Apple has to offer.

Apple Pay and Wallet

One of the most convenient and widely used services in Apple's ecosystem is Apple Pay, a contactless payment system that allows you to pay for goods and services using your iPhone. The Wallet app also stores more than just payment methods—you can add transit cards, credit cards, debit cards, tickets, boarding passes, and even ID cards, making it an essential tool for both daily and special occasions.

1. Setting Up Apple Pay

Apple Pay is available in many countries and can be set up easily with any major credit or debit card. Here's how to get started.

How to Set Up Apple Pay:

1. Open the Wallet App: Find the Wallet app on your Home Screen or use the Search function to locate it.

2. Add a Card: Tap the + symbol in the upper-right corner of the screen to add a new card.

3. Choose Card Type: Select whether you're adding a debit or credit card.

4. Scan or Enter Your Card Details: Use your iPhone's camera to scan your card, or manually enter your card information, including the card number, expiration date, and CVV.

5. Verify with Your Bank: Depending on your bank, you may need to verify your card via text, email, or phone call.

6. Ready to Use: Once verified, your card will appear in the Wallet app, and you're ready to start using Apple Pay.

How to Use Apple Pay:

To make a purchase using Apple Pay:

1. Unlock Your iPhone: Double-press the side button (or use Face ID/Touch ID, depending on your iPhone model) when you're ready to pay.

2. Hold Near the Payment Terminal: Once your default card appears on the screen, hold your iPhone near the contactless payment terminal.

3. Authenticate: Use Face ID, Touch ID, or your passcode to complete the payment.

Apple Pay works in stores that accept contactless payments, as well as within apps and online. When shopping online, look for the Apple Pay logo during checkout for a fast, secure payment experience without needing to enter your card details manually.

2. Using Apple Wallet for Transit Cards, Tickets, and More

The Wallet app goes beyond just payments. It can store a wide range of digital cards, from transit passes and event tickets to boarding passes and ID cards in supported regions.

Adding Transit Cards:

If you live in a city where Apple Pay supports transit systems, you can add your transit card to the Wallet app for quick and convenient travel.

1. Open the Wallet App.

2. Tap the + symbol and select Transit Card.

3. Choose your city or transit system from the list, then follow the prompts to add a card. You can either add an existing card or create a new one and load it with funds.

4. To use the card, double-press the side button and hold your iPhone near the transit terminal, just as you would with a physical card.

Adding Event Tickets and Boarding Passes:

Tickets for concerts, movies, and flights can also be stored in Wallet, making it easy to manage your passes.

- **Through Email or Apps:** When you purchase tickets online or through an app (e.g., Ticketmaster, airline apps), you'll often be given the option to add them to Apple Wallet directly.

- QR Codes: Some vendors allow you to scan a QR code sent via email or text, which will then import the ticket into Wallet.

Once added, you can simply open Wallet at the venue or airport, tap the ticket, and scan your iPhone for entry.

Digital ID Cards:

In some regions, Apple Wallet now supports adding digital driver's licenses and state IDs. This feature allows you to securely store your identification on your iPhone, and it can be used in places where digital IDs are accepted.

Apple Music, TV+, Arcade, and Fitness+

Apple offers a wide range of subscription-based services to meet your entertainment and fitness needs. Each of these services is designed to integrate with the iPhone 16, providing access to a vast library of content and personalized experiences.

1. Apple Music

Apple Music is a streaming service that offers access to over 90 million songs, curated playlists, and exclusive content. Whether you're a casual listener or a music enthusiast, Apple Music provides an ad-free listening experience with offline downloads and personalized recommendations.

Key Features:

- **Personalized Playlists:** Apple Music creates daily personalized playlists like Favorites Mix, New Music Mix, and Chill Mix, tailored to your listening preferences.

- Lossless Audio and Spatial Audio: Enjoy higher-quality sound with Lossless Audio, and experience Spatial Audio for an immersive, 3D-like listening experience with compatible headphones.

- Offline Playback: You can download songs, albums, and playlists to listen offline, making it perfect for commutes or traveling.

Maximizing Your Experience:

- Sync Your Library: If you have songs purchased or uploaded from other sources, you can sync them to your Apple Music library across all devices using iCloud Music Library.

- Discover New Music: Explore curated playlists and the Browse section to find new songs, artists, and genres you may not have heard before.

2. Apple TV+

Apple TV+ is Apple's streaming service for original movies, documentaries, and TV series. With award-winning content such as Ted Lasso, The Morning

Show, and Severance, Apple TV+ provides ad-free entertainment at a low monthly subscription cost.

Key Features:

- **Exclusive Originals:** Access Apple's growing library of original programming, including documentaries, dramas, comedies, and more.

- **Download for Offline Viewing:** Apple TV+ allows you to download content for offline viewing, making it ideal for travel or areas with poor internet connectivity.

- **Apple One Bundle:** You can get Apple TV+ as part of the Apple One bundle, which includes multiple Apple services at a discounted rate.

Maximizing Your Experience:

- **Watch Anywhere:** Apple TV+ integrates with the Apple TV app, which is available on a variety of platforms, including smart TVs, gaming consoles, and even some streaming devices, so you can watch your favorite shows anywhere.

- **Family Sharing:** Share your Apple TV+ subscription with up to five family members using Family Sharing at no additional cost.

3. Apple Arcade

For gamers, Apple Arcade provides access to over 200 premium, ad-free games, playable across iPhone, iPad, Mac, and Apple TV. With a subscription to Apple Arcade, you gain access to high-quality games without in-app purchases or ads.

Key Features:

- **No Ads or In-App Purchases:** Enjoy a distraction-free gaming experience where you never have to worry about paywalls or interruptions.

- **Cross-Device Play:** Start a game on your iPhone and continue playing on your iPad, Mac, or Apple TV seamlessly, thanks to cross-device support.

- **Controller Support:** Many Apple Arcade games support third-party controllers, such as PlayStation and Xbox controllers, for a more console-like experience.

Maximizing Your Experience:

- **Explore Categories:** Apple Arcade organizes games into categories like Action, Puzzle, Family, and more, so you can easily find new games based on your preferences.

- **Offline Play:** You can download Apple Arcade games for offline play, making it convenient for long trips or areas with limited internet access.

4. Apple Fitness+

Apple Fitness+ is Apple's subscription service designed to integrate with the Apple Watch to deliver personalized fitness content. It offers guided workouts, meditations, and programs led by professional trainers, all of which sync with your workout data on the iPhone, iPad, or Apple TV.

Key Features:

- Real-Time Metrics: When using Apple Fitness+ with an Apple Watch, you can see real-time metrics like heart rate, calories burned, and activity rings directly on the screen during a workout.

- Wide Range of Workouts: Choose from a variety of workout types, including HIIT, Yoga, Core, Strength, and Dance, with new workouts added weekly.

- Guided Meditations: Apple Fitness+ also offers Mindfulness Meditations to help you relax, focus, and improve your mental health.

Maximizing Your Experience:

- Tailored Workouts: Fitness+ offers Beginner, Intermediate, and Advanced workouts, allowing you to find routines that match your fitness level.

- Workout Anywhere: Whether you're at home, in the gym, or on the go, you can stream Fitness+ workouts from your iPhone, iPad, or Apple TV.

iCloud+ and Private Relay

iCloud+ is Apple's premium iCloud subscription that expands the functionality of its cloud storage service with additional privacy and security features. In addition to more storage, iCloud+ includes Private Relay and Hide My Email, giving users greater control over their online activities and personal information.

1. Private Relay

Private Relay is an iCloud+ feature designed to protect your browsing activity by encrypting your internet traffic. It works by routing your Internet traffic through two separate servers, ensuring that neither Apple nor any website can track your browsing behavior or IP address.

How Private Relay Works:

- **First Server (Apple):** *The first server encrypts your browsing data and strips your IP address from the request.*

- Second Server (Third Party): The second server assigns you a new, temporary IP address before sending the request to the website you're trying to access.

This two-step process ensures that your identity and location are protected while you browse the internet, making Private Relay an excellent feature for users concerned about privacy.

Enabling Private Relay:

1. Go to Settings > [Your Name] > iCloud > Private Relay.

2. Toggle on Private Relay.

Private Relay is designed to work automatically, protecting your browsing data without requiring any manual intervention.

2. Hide My Email

Hide My Email is another powerful privacy feature offered by iCloud+. It allows you to create randomized, unique email addresses that forward messages to your real inbox. This is particularly useful when signing up for newsletters, creating accounts, or using services that may share your email address with third parties.

Key Features:

- **Randomized Emails:** When you sign up for a new service or website, you can generate a unique email address that forwards messages to your real email, protecting your identity.

- **Manage Forwarding Addresses:** You can view and delete these email addresses at any time if you no longer wish to receive messages from a particular service.

How to Use Hide My Email:

1. Go to Settings > [Your Name] > iCloud > Hide My Email.

2. Tap Create New Address to generate a random email address.

3. Use this address when signing up for services, and emails will be forwarded to your inbox.

You can manage and delete these email aliases at any time, giving you more control over which companies have access to your real email address.

Apple's suite of services, from Apple Pay and Apple Music to iCloud+ and Private Relay, transforms the iPhone 16 into a powerful tool for payments, entertainment, fitness, and privacy. With Apple Pay, you can enjoy fast, contactless payments and store everything from transit cards to boarding passes in your Wallet. Apple's entertainment offerings—Music, TV+, Arcade, and Fitness+—provide a seamless multimedia experience tailored to your interests and lifestyle. Finally, iCloud+ and its privacy features ensure that your data remains secure, whether you're storing files or protecting your online activity with Private Relay. By mastering these services, you can take full advantage of the iPhone 16's capabilities and enjoy a seamless, secure experience across all aspects of your digital life.

CHAPTER 12

ACCESSIBILITY FEATURES

*****

Apple has always prioritized inclusivity, and the iPhone 16 is no exception. Packed with an array of accessibility features, it caters to users with different abilities, ensuring that everyone can enjoy a seamless experience. From vision and hearing assistance to tools like AssistiveTouch and motion control, these features are designed to provide users with the flexibility and support they need to navigate and interact with their devices. This chapter will cover how to access and use key accessibility settings such as VoiceOver, Magnifier, audio accommodations, and more, making the iPhone 16 a powerful tool for users with unique needs.

Vision and Hearing Assistance

Apple's accessibility features for vision and hearing aim to ensure that users with impairments can use their devices with ease. Whether you're navigating your iPhone's interface, making calls, or reading documents, features like VoiceOver, Magnifier, and audio accommodations can significantly improve your experience.

1. VoiceOver

VoiceOver is one of Apple's most powerful accessibility tools. It is a screen reader that allows users to hear a description of everything happening on their screen. From reading text aloud to describing images and buttons, VoiceOver makes the iPhone 16 fully accessible to users with vision impairments.

How to Enable VoiceOver:

1. Open Settings: Navigate to Settings > Accessibility > VoiceOver.

2. Toggle On VoiceOver: Once activated, VoiceOver will immediately begin describing the items on your screen.

3. Customize Settings: VoiceOver allows for various customization options, such as adjusting the speaking rate, choosing different voices, or enabling Braille displays.

Using VoiceOver:

- **Navigating the Screen:** Once VoiceOver is enabled, you'll interact with your iPhone differently. You can tap anywhere on the screen, and VoiceOver will describe what's under your finger. Double-tap to select an item, and swipe with three fingers to scroll through lists or pages.

- **Rotor Feature:** VoiceOver includes a unique rotor feature, which lets you change how you navigate content. Rotate two fingers on the screen like a dial to switch between options like words, characters, or links, depending on the context of the content you're reading or interacting with.

- Braille Support: VoiceOver also works with Braille displays, providing support for more than 70 international Braille tables. You can connect a Bluetooth Braille display to your iPhone for real-time feedback.

Customizing VoiceOver Gestures:

VoiceOver comes with a range of gestures that allow you to interact with your iPhone in new ways. If you're more comfortable with certain gestures or need adjustments, you can customize them:

1. Settings > Accessibility > VoiceOver > Commands.

2. From here, you can assign different actions to gestures or even use keyboard shortcuts if you have an external keyboard.

VoiceOver is a comprehensive tool that gives visually impaired users complete control over their iPhones. It works seamlessly across Apple's apps and even extends to third-party apps that support accessibility.

2. Magnifier

For users who need visual assistance but may not require a screen reader, the Magnifier tool is an invaluable resource. Magnifier turns your iPhone into a digital magnifying glass, helping you enlarge text, objects, and images in your environment.

How to Enable Magnifier:

1. Open Settings: Go to Settings > Accessibility > Magnifier.

2. Toggle On Magnifier: Once enabled, the Magnifier can be accessed from the Control Center or by triple-clicking the side button.

Using Magnifier:

- **Adjust Magnification:** Open the Magnifier through the Control Center or by pressing the side button, then use the on-screen slider to adjust the zoom level. You can zoom in on text or objects up to 15x for better clarity.

- **Apply Filters:** Magnifier also includes filters that can adjust the contrast or color balance to enhance visibility. Choose between Grayscale, Red/Black, or Yellow/Black filters, depending on your preferences.

- **Freeze Frame:** Magnifier includes a freeze frame function that lets you capture an image and magnify it later without holding your iPhone over the object. This is especially useful for reading labels, small text, or intricate details.

- **Flashlight Integration:** If you're using Magnifier in a low-light environment, you can also turn on your iPhone's flashlight for better visibility.

A magnifier is ideal for anyone who occasionally needs visual assistance for reading fine print, inspecting small objects, or navigating low-light environments.

3. Audio Accommodations

Apple has built several audio accommodations into the iPhone 16 to enhance the experience for users with hearing impairments. These features include Hearing Aids Compatibility, Mono Audio, Live Listen, and more.

Hearing Aids Compatibility:

The iPhone 16 is compatible with Made for iPhone (MFi) hearing aids, allowing users to stream audio directly from their iPhone to their hearing aids, making calls and media playback clearer and easier to hear.

How to Pair Your Hearing Aids:

1. Go to Settings > Accessibility > Hearing Devices.

2. Turn on your hearing aids and make sure Bluetooth is enabled on your iPhone.

3. Tap your hearing aids under the Hearing Devices section to pair them.

Once connected, you can control your hearing aids directly from your iPhone. This includes adjusting volume levels, switching between audio presets, or even using Live Listen, a feature that turns your iPhone into a remote microphone to amplify sound in noisy environments.

Mono Audio:

If you have hearing loss in one ear, Mono Audio ensures that both the left and right channels of stereo audio are played in both ears, so you don't miss any part of the conversation or music.

How to Enable Mono Audio:

1. Go to Settings > Accessibility > Audio/Visual.

2. Toggle on Mono Audio.

Live Listen:

Live Listen uses your iPhone's microphone to pick up sound and transmit it directly to your AirPods, AirPods Pro, or hearing aids. This is particularly helpful in crowded or noisy environments where hearing clarity is reduced.

How to Activate Live Listen:

1. Go to Settings > Control Center and add Hearing to Control Center.

2. Open the Control Center and tap the Hearing icon.

3. Tap Live Listen to begin using your iPhone's microphone to amplify sound.

Whether you're using hearing aids, AirPods, or other supported audio devices, Apple's accommodations provide excellent support for those with hearing impairments.

AssistiveTouch and Motion

For users with limited mobility or dexterity challenges, Apple offers AssistiveTouch and other features that reduce the need for physical interaction with the screen. These tools allow users to control their iPhones through on-screen gestures, external devices, or even voice commands.

1. AssistiveTouch

AssistiveTouch is a customizable on-screen menu that enables users to perform gestures and actions without having to use physical buttons. This feature is essential for individuals who find it difficult to interact with their iPhones through traditional methods like tapping, swiping, or pressing buttons.

How to Enable AssistiveTouch:

1. Open Settings: Go to Settings > Accessibility > Touch > AssistiveTouch.

2. Toggle On AssistiveTouch: Once activated, a floating button will appear on your screen.

Customizing AssistiveTouch:

- Actions: Tap the floating AssistiveTouch button to access a menu of customizable actions, such as Home, Control Center, Screenshot, or Notifications. You can add or remove actions based on your preferences and assign gestures to single-tap, double-tap, long press, or 3D Touch actions.

- Gestures: AssistiveTouch supports gestures like pinching and swiping, which can be difficult for some users to perform physically. You can create custom gestures by recording touch patterns, which AssistiveTouch will replicate when activated.

- Device Controls: AssistiveTouch also includes controls for hardware features such as adjusting the volume, locking the screen, rotating the display, and accessing Siri without pressing any physical buttons.

AssistiveTouch and External Devices:

AssistiveTouch can be paired with external hardware such as Bluetooth keyboards or adaptive switches. These accessories allow users to control their iPhones using a physical switch, joystick, or other assistive devices, making it possible to navigate the iPhone without touching the screen.

2. Motion Settings

Apple's accessibility features include motion control options to accommodate users who are sensitive to motion or prefer alternative ways of interacting with their devices.

Reduce Motion:

The Reduce Motion feature limits the visual animations and transitions that occur when opening apps or switching between screens. Some users may experience discomfort or disorientation with these effects, and enabling Reduce Motion creates a more stationary user interface.

How to Enable Reduce Motion:

1. Go to Settings > Accessibility > Motion.

2. Toggle on Reduce Motion.

Once activated, Reduce Motion disables features like the parallax effect (where the background moves slightly as you tilt the phone) and zooming transitions between apps, creating a simpler experience.

Shake to Undo:

The Shake to Undo feature allows users to undo the last action (such as typing) by physically shaking the iPhone. While this can be useful, it can also be accidentally triggered. If you find this feature difficult to use, you can turn it off.

How to Disable Shake to Undo:

1. Go to Settings > Accessibility > Touch.

2. Toggle off

Shake to Undo.

Reachability:

For users with smaller hands or mobility limitations, Reachability makes it easier to reach the top of the screen by lowering the entire interface with a simple gesture.

How to Enable Reachability:

1. Go to Settings > Accessibility > Touch.

2. Toggle on Reachability.

To activate Reachability, swipe down on the bottom edge of the screen. This will bring the top portion of the screen down, allowing you to reach items more easily.

The iPhone 16's extensive range of accessibility features ensures that it remains one of the most inclusive smartphones on the market. From VoiceOver and Magnifier for vision support to audio accommodations like Live Listen and AssistiveTouch for those with mobility needs, Apple's commitment to accessibility is evident in every facet of the device's design. By learning how to customize these features, users with unique challenges can tailor their iPhone experience to suit their individual needs, empowering them to enjoy all the benefits of modern technology.

CHAPTER 13

TROUBLESHOOTING AND MAINTENANCE

*****

Even with its advanced technology and robust software, the iPhone 16 can occasionally encounter problems that affect performance. Whether you're dealing with Wi-Fi issues, app crashes, or an unresponsive screen, understanding how to troubleshoot and maintain your device is essential for keeping it running smoothly. In this chapter, we will provide practical solutions for common issues, walk you through the process of resetting and restoring your iPhone, and explain how to manage iOS updates to ensure your device stays up to date.

Common Issues and Fixes

Every iPhone user may face some technical hiccups from time to time, but most issues are easily resolved with basic troubleshooting steps. Below are some of the most frequent problems users encounter and how to fix them.

1. Wi-Fi Issues

A reliable Wi-Fi connection is crucial for most iPhone functions, from browsing the internet to downloading apps. If your iPhone is having trouble connecting to Wi-Fi, try the following steps to troubleshoot.

Problem: iPhone Won't Connect to Wi-Fi

- **Check Your Wi-Fi Network:** First, ensure your Wi-Fi is working on other devices. If your router is malfunctioning, it could be a network issue rather than an iPhone problem.

- **Toggle Wi-Fi Off and On:** Sometimes simply turning Wi-Fi off and back on can solve the problem. Go to Settings > Wi-Fi and toggle the switch.

- Forget the Network: If you're unable to connect, try "forgetting" the network and reconnecting:

1. Go to Settings > Wi-Fi.

2. Tap the i next to the network you're trying to connect to.

3. Tap Forget This Network, then reconnect by entering your Wi-Fi password.

- Reset Network Settings: If the problem persists, resetting your network settings may help:

1. Go to Settings > General > Transfer or Reset iPhone.

2. Tap Reset, then select Reset Network Settings.

This will clear all saved Wi-Fi passwords, so you'll need to re-enter them after the reset.

Problem: Slow or Unstable Wi-Fi Connection

- **Move Closer to the Router:** Sometimes distance or obstacles can interfere with your connection. Ensure that you're within range of your Wi-Fi router.

- **Disable Background App Refresh:** Apps running in the background can slow down your Wi-Fi speed. Go to Settings > General > Background App Refresh and turn it off for non-essential apps.

- **Check for Interference:** Other devices like microwaves, Bluetooth devices, or even other Wi-Fi networks can interfere with your signal. Switching your router to a different channel or frequency (such as 5 GHz instead of 2.4 GHz) might improve your connection.

2. App Crashes

Occasionally, apps may crash or freeze, disrupting your work or entertainment. Here's how to troubleshoot when apps aren't working as expected.

Problem: An App Keeps Crashing

- **Force Close the App:** Double-press the Home button (or swipe up from the bottom of the screen on Face ID models) to open the App Switcher. Swipe the app upward to close it. Reopen the app to see if the issue is resolved.

- **Update the App:** Go to the App Store and check if there's an update available for the app. App updates often include bug fixes that can resolve crashes.

- **Restart Your iPhone:** Restarting your iPhone can clear temporary glitches that may cause an app to crash.

- **Delete and Reinstall the App:** If the app continues to crash, try deleting it and reinstalling it from the App Store. This will clear any corrupted data associated with the app.

- **Check App Permissions:** Some apps require access to certain functions (like the camera or microphone). Go to Settings > Privacy and ensure the app has the necessary permissions.

3. Unresponsive Screen

If your iPhone's screen becomes unresponsive, there are a few quick fixes to try before seeking professional help.

Problem: The Screen is Frozen or Unresponsive

- Force Restart Your iPhone:

1. Press and quickly release the Volume Up button.

2. Press and quickly release the Volume Down button.

3. Press and hold the Side button until the Apple logo appears.

This force restart should resolve any temporary software issues causing the screen to freeze.

- **Clean the Screen:** Sometimes dirt, debris, or even moisture on the screen can cause it to be unresponsive. Clean your screen with a soft, dry cloth and see if that improves responsiveness.

- Remove the Case or Screen Protector: In some cases, a poorly fitted screen protector or case can interfere with touch sensitivity. Try removing these and testing the screen again.

4. Battery Draining Quickly

If you notice that your battery is draining faster than usual, some adjustments can help extend battery life.

Problem: Rapid Battery Drain

- Check Battery Usage: Go to Settings > Battery to see which apps are consuming the most power. If an app is using an abnormal amount of battery, consider limiting its use or uninstalling it.

- Turn Off Background App Refresh: Disabling background app activity can help preserve battery life. Go to Settings > General > Background App Refresh.

- Enable Low Power Mode: Low Power Mode reduces battery drain by disabling non-essential features. You can activate it from Settings > Battery or through Control Center.

- Adjust Display Settings: Reducing screen brightness or enabling Auto-Brightness can help conserve power. Go to Settings > Display & Brightness to make adjustments.

- Update iOS: Occasionally, iOS updates include fixes for battery issues. Go to Settings > General > Software Update to ensure you're running the latest version of iOS.

Resetting and Restoring

If basic troubleshooting doesn't resolve your iPhone's issues, more advanced methods like resetting or restoring the device may be necessary. A reset can help fix many common software-related problems, while a full restore returns your iPhone to its factory settings, erasing all data in the process.

1. Resetting Your iPhone

Resetting your iPhone doesn't erase all your data but clears specific settings that might be causing issues. Apple offers several types of resets depending on the problem you're facing.

Types of Resets:

- **Reset All Settings:** This option clears system settings (like Wi-Fi networks, display settings, and privacy settings) but keeps your data intact.

1. Go to Settings > General > Transfer or Reset iPhone.

2. Tap Reset, then select Reset All Settings.

- Reset Network Settings: This resets your Wi-Fi, Bluetooth, and VPN settings, which can help with connectivity issues.

1. Go to Settings > General > Transfer or Reset iPhone.

2. Tap Reset, then select Reset Network Settings.

- Reset Keyboard Dictionary: If your iPhone's predictive text is problematic, you can reset the keyboard dictionary to start fresh.

1. Go to Settings > General > Transfer or Reset iPhone.

2. Tap Reset, then select Reset Keyboard Dictionary.

2. Restoring Your iPhone

If your iPhone continues to have significant problems after trying to reset, you may need to restore it to factory settings. Restoring will erase all data, apps, and settings, so be sure to back up your device before proceeding.

How to Perform a Full Restore:

1. Back Up Your iPhone: Before restoring, it's essential to back up your iPhone via iCloud or Finder (on macOS) or iTunes (on Windows). Go to Settings > [Your Name] > iCloud > iCloud Backup and select Back Up Now to ensure all your data is safe.

2. Go to Settings > General > Transfer or Reset iPhone.

3. Tap Erase All Content and Settings. You'll need to enter your passcode and Apple ID password to confirm.

4. Restore from Backup: Once the restore is complete, you can set up your iPhone as a new device or restore it from an iCloud or iTunes/Finder backup to retrieve your data.

If the restore doesn't resolve the issue, it may be a hardware problem, and contacting Apple Support for repair or replacement may be necessary.

Software Updates

Keeping your iPhone up to date with the latest iOS software is one of the best ways to avoid problems and ensure that your device is running smoothly. Apple regularly releases updates that include bug fixes, security enhancements, and new features.

1. Checking for Software Updates

To check if an update is available:

1. Open Settings: Go to Settings > General > Software Update.

2. Your iPhone will automatically check for updates. If one is available, tap Download and Install.

Make sure you're connected to Wi-Fi and have at least 50% battery (or are plugged into a charger) before updating. Software updates can take a few minutes to an hour depending on the size of the update and your internet connection.

2. Enabling Automatic Updates

You can set your iPhone to automatically download and install iOS updates, ensuring that your device is always up to date.

How to Enable Automatic Updates:

1. Go to Settings > General > Software Update > Automatic Updates.

2. Toggle on Download iOS Updates and Install iOS Updates.

When automatic updates are enabled, your iPhone will download and install updates overnight while charging, ensuring that you don't experience interruptions during the day.

3. Managing Storage for Updates

Sometimes, you may run into an issue where there isn't enough storage to install an update. If this happens, here's how to manage your storage.

Freeing Up Space for an Update:

1. Go to Settings > General > iPhone Storage.

2. Review the list of apps to see how much space they are using. Delete any apps or large files you no longer need.

3. You can also enable Offload Unused Apps, which removes apps you haven't used in a while but keeps their data intact for easy reinstallation.

Troubleshooting and maintaining your iPhone 16 is crucial for a smooth user experience. Whether you're dealing with Wi-Fi connectivity issues, app crashes, or battery problems, the most common issues can be resolved with basic troubleshooting steps. If needed, you can always perform resets or even a full restore to get your device back in top shape. Regularly updating iOS and managing storage ensures your iPhone stays secure and optimized. By mastering these troubleshooting and maintenance techniques, you'll keep your iPhone running efficiently and minimize any disruptions to your digital life.

CHAPTER 14

ADVANCED TIPS AND TRICKS

*****

The iPhone 16 is packed with powerful features that extend far beyond the basics of making calls, browsing the web, or sending messages. For advanced users looking to optimize their experience, there are numerous tools and techniques available to enhance productivity and customization. From automating tasks with the Shortcuts app to mastering multitasking features, and even diving deep into customization options, this chapter will walk you through advanced tips and tricks that can transform how you use your iPhone.

Shortcuts App: Automating Tasks and Enhancing Productivity

The Shortcuts app is one of the most powerful tools on the iPhone 16, allowing you to automate repetitive tasks, streamline workflows, and control apps with custom commands. Whether you're creating simple shortcuts for personal use or designing complex multi-step automation, the Shortcuts app can significantly boost your productivity.

1. Introduction to the Shortcuts App

Shortcuts allow you to create automated actions and routines that can be triggered with a single tap or voice command using Siri. These actions can interact with built-in apps, third-party apps, and even system settings, making it a versatile tool for saving time and effort.

How to Create a Basic Shortcut:

1. Open the Shortcuts app on your iPhone.

2. Tap the + icon in the top-right corner to create a new shortcut.

3. Tap Add Action to choose the first step of your shortcut. For example, you can choose to send a message, open an app, or play a specific song.

4. Once the action is selected, you can customize it (e.g., specifying the message recipient or the song title).

5. Tap Add Action again to add more steps if needed. You can chain multiple actions together, such as turning on Wi-Fi, setting a timer, and playing music when you arrive home.

6. After adding all actions, tap Next, give your shortcut a name, and tap Done to save it.

Once created, your shortcut can be accessed from the Shortcuts app, the Home Screen, or triggered via Siri.

Examples of Useful Shortcuts:

- **Morning Routine:** A shortcut that turns off Do Not Disturb, checks your calendar, and plays your favorite morning playlist.

- **Send ETA:** A shortcut that sends your estimated time of arrival (ETA) to a contact when you're on your way to meet them.

- **Home Automation:** A shortcut that turns off the lights, locks the doors, and activates Low Power Mode when you leave the house.

2. Using Automations in Shortcuts

In addition to one-tap shortcuts, the Automations feature in the Shortcuts app allows you to set up tasks that trigger automatically based on conditions, such as time of day, location, or app usage.

How to Set Up Automation:

1. Open the Shortcuts app and tap the Automation tab at the bottom.

2. Tap Create Personal Automation.

3. Choose the trigger for your automation. For example, you can choose the Time of Day to create a routine that runs every morning or Arrive to trigger actions when you arrive at a specific location.

4. Add the actions you want to be executed when the trigger occurs. For instance, you might turn on your lights and start a playlist when you arrive home.

5. Tap Next, then Done to activate your automation.

Automations are highly customizable, allowing you to create workflows that adapt to your daily routines seamlessly.

3. Advanced Shortcuts Techniques

For those seeking more complexity, Shortcuts offers advanced options such as:

- **Variables:** Variables allow you to store data (such as text or numbers) and use it later in your shortcut.

For example, you can store the current date in a variable and include it in a message sent later.

- **Conditional Logic:** Use If statements to create shortcuts that change their behavior based on certain conditions. For example, you can create a shortcut that sends a different message based on whether you are at work or home.

By mastering the Shortcuts app, you can automate your iPhone to fit your lifestyle, reducing the number of manual steps required for your day-to-day tasks.

Multitasking Features

The iPhone 16 introduces a variety of multitasking features that allow you to easily switch between apps, perform multiple tasks at once, and manage multiple types of media in a more streamlined manner. These tools include Picture-in-Picture, drag-and-drop, and app-switching techniques.

1. Picture-in-Picture (PiP)

Picture-in-Picture allows you to continue watching videos or participating in FaceTime calls while using other apps. This feature shrinks the video into a small, resizable window that floats over your Home Screen or other open apps, giving you the flexibility to multitask.

How to Use Picture-in-Picture:

1. Start playing a video in an app that supports PiP (such as Safari, Apple TV, or FaceTime).

2. Swipe up from the bottom of the screen (or press the Home button) to return to the Home Screen. The video will shrink into a small floating window.

3. You can drag the PiP window to any corner of the screen or resize it by pinching it with two fingers.

4. To return the video to full screen, tap the PiP window and then tap the full-screen icon in the top-right corner.

This feature is especially useful for tasks like watching a tutorial while following instructions in another app or staying on a FaceTime call while responding to messages.

2. Drag-and-Drop Between Apps

The iPhone 16 supports drag-and-drop functionality, which allows you to move content like text, photos, or files from one app to another. This feature enhances productivity by eliminating the need to copy and paste content manually.

How to Use Drag-and-Drop:

1. Open an app where you want to drag content from (e.g., Photos, Safari, or Notes).

2. Touch and hold the content you want to drag (such as an image, block of text, or file) until it lifts from the screen.

3. Without releasing, use another finger to swipe up and open another app where you want to drop the content.

4. Drag the content to the desired location in the second app and release it.

For example, you can drag a photo from Photos and drop it directly into a conversation in Messages or a document in Notes.

3. App Switching and Split View (on iPad)

While the iPhone does not support Split View like the iPad, it still offers efficient app-switching features. Knowing how to quickly switch between apps and manage your open applications can boost productivity.

How to Switch Between Apps:

- Swipe Gesture: On Face ID models, swipe left or right along the bottom of the screen to quickly switch between recently used apps.

- App Switcher: To access the App Switcher, swipe up from the bottom of the screen and pause in the middle (or double-click the Home button on older models). This view shows all your open apps, and you can swipe through them to select or close apps by swiping them upward.

Using these multitasking tools makes it easier to juggle multiple tasks, such as referencing information in one app while working on another.

Advanced Customization Options

One of the strengths of the iPhone 16 is its ability to be deeply customized. From organizing your Home Screen to creating personalized ringtones, advanced customization features give you full control over how your iPhone looks and feels.

1. Customizing the Home Screen

With iOS 16, Apple introduced more flexibility in customizing the Home Screen, including options to rearrange app icons, create custom widgets, and design a Home Screen that matches your style and workflow.

Rearranging App Icons:

- To rearrange apps, tap and hold an app icon until it enters jiggle mode.

- Drag the app to a new position on the Home Screen or into a folder.

- You can also move apps between Home Screen pages by dragging them to the edge of the screen.

Creating Custom Widgets:

Widgets provide at-a-glance information from your favorite apps, and you can now add customized widgets directly to your Home Screen.

1. Tap and hold anywhere on the Home Screen until the icons start to jiggle.

2. Tap the + icon in the top-left corner to open the widget gallery.

3. Browse the available widgets and tap one to add it to your Home Screen.

4. You can resize widgets and stack multiple widgets on top of each other to create Smart Stacks, which rotate based on your activity or time of day.

Customizing your Home Screen layout with widgets and folders makes it easier to access the apps and information you use most frequently.

2. Changing App Icons

If you want a truly personalized Home Screen, you can change the icons for your apps using the Shortcuts app. This allows you to create a theme for your Home Screen by replacing default app icons with custom designs.

How to Change App Icons:

1. Open the Shortcuts app and tap + to create a new shortcut.

2. Tap Add Action, then search for Open App.

3. Tap Choose, then select the app you want to customize.

4. Tap the three dots in the upper-right corner, then tap Add to Home Screen.

5. Tap the default icon to change it, then choose an image from your Photos or Files.

6. Rename the shortcut to match the app's name, then tap Add.

Your custom icon will appear on the Home Screen. Repeat this process for each app you want to customize.

3. Creating Custom Ringtones

You can create and set custom ringtones for calls, texts, and other alerts. While Apple offers a variety of default ringtones, you can use music or audio clips to make your iPhone's sounds truly unique.

How to Create Custom Ringtones:

1. Download the GarageBand app from the App Store if you don't already have it installed.

2. Open GarageBand and select Audio Recorder.

3. Tap the + icon in the top-right corner to set the length of the ringtone (it should be 30 seconds or less).

4. Import your chosen audio file (such as a song or sound effect) and trim it as needed.

5. Tap the share icon and select Ringtone. Give your ringtone a name and export it.

6. Once the ringtone is saved, go to Settings > Sounds & Haptics > Ringtone and select your custom ringtone.

This gives your iPhone a more personal touch, as you can set different ringtones for specific contacts or events.

Mastering the advanced tips and tricks available on the iPhone 16 can unlock a new level of productivity, convenience, and customization. By automating tasks with the Shortcuts app, taking advantage of multitasking features like Picture-in-Picture and drag-and-drop, and diving into advanced customization options such as changing app icons and creating custom ringtones, you can truly tailor your iPhone experience to your personal preferences and needs. Whether you're a power user looking to streamline your workflow or simply someone who enjoys personalizing your device, these tips will help you maximize the potential of your iPhone 16.

CHAPTER 15

MAXIMIZING YOUR IPHONE EXPERIENCE

*****

The iPhone 16 is more than just a communication device—it's a powerful tool that can boost productivity, streamline workflows, enhance gaming, and even automate daily tasks. Whether you're a professional looking to use the iPhone for work or a gamer eager to elevate your experience, there are a variety of third-party apps and built-in features that can help you get the most out of your device. In this chapter, we will explore advanced apps for power users, provide a comprehensive guide on using the iPhone for work, and offer tips on enhancing your gaming performance to ensure you're maximizing every aspect of your iPhone experience.

Third-Party Apps for Power Users

While Apple's native apps cover most day-to-day tasks, there's a world of third-party apps designed for power users looking to go beyond the basics. From task managers that boost productivity to photo editors that offer professional-grade tools, these apps can enhance your workflow and give you more control over your iPhone experience.

1. Task Managers

For users juggling multiple projects, appointments, and deadlines, advanced task management apps can significantly improve organization and efficiency. While Apple's Reminders app is functional, there are more powerful third-party options with greater flexibility.

Recommended Task Manager Apps:

- **Things 3:** A highly intuitive task manager that offers a clean design, powerful organizational tools, and seamless sync across Apple devices. You can create projects, set deadlines, add tags, and organize tasks into sections like Today, Upcoming, and Someday. With the ability to schedule tasks and break them down into smaller steps, Things 3 is perfect for users who want to manage complex workflows.

- **Todoist:** A versatile task manager that integrates with other productivity tools like Google Calendar and Slack. Todoist's interface is simple but powerful, with features like project prioritization, natural language task entry, and task delegation for team-based workflows. Its robust reminder system ensures you stay on top of everything.

- **OmniFocus:** A more advanced option for professionals, OmniFocus is ideal for users who rely on GTD (Getting Things Done) methodology. Its unique organizational structure includes projects, contexts, perspectives, and flags, allowing for granular task management. With features like location-based reminders and customizable views, OmniFocus is a must-have for power users.

2. Photo Editing Tools

Whether you're an amateur photographer or a professional creative, the iPhone 16's camera is capable of capturing stunning photos. However, to take full advantage of its capabilities, third-party photo editing apps offer advanced features like RAW editing, filters, and retouching tools.

Recommended Photo Editing Apps:

- **Adobe Lightroom:** For photographers looking to edit RAW files or apply detailed adjustments to their photos, Lightroom is one of the best options available. It provides tools for exposure, color correction, and noise reduction, as well as the ability to sync edits across devices with Adobe Creative Cloud integration. Its non-destructive editing process ensures you can always revert to your original images.

- **VSCO:** A popular app for casual and professional photographers alike, VSCO offers a variety of presets that give your photos a professional finish with minimal effort. Its advanced editing tools allow you to fine-tune exposure, contrast, and color balance, while the community aspect provides inspiration and creative challenges.

- Darkroom: For users who want a blend of simplicity and power, Darkroom offers both advanced photo and video editing features. With a wide array of color correction tools, including curves and selective color adjustments, Darkroom is perfect for those who want to edit with precision without the steep learning curve of more complex software.

3. Automation Tools

Power users looking to automate repetitive tasks and streamline their daily workflows will benefit from apps designed for automation. Beyond Apple's built-in Shortcuts app, there are third-party solutions that offer even more versatility and depth.

Recommended Automation Apps:

- IFTTT (If This Then That): IFTTT is a powerful tool for automating tasks across apps and devices. It lets you create "applets" that connect different services, such as sending a text message when you leave work or automatically posting Instagram photos to Twitter. With support for over 700 apps and smart devices, IFTTT can automate nearly every aspect of your digital life.

- **Launch Center Pro:** This app helps you automate repetitive actions by creating quick-access shortcuts for tasks like sending pre-written messages, posting to social media, or even performing complex multi-step actions. It also integrates with many popular apps, enabling you to trigger specific actions with just a few taps.

- **Pushcut:** Pushcut is designed to enhance Shortcuts by adding conditions and advanced triggers. You can create workflows that trigger based on specific events, time of day, or location. It's a great app for users who want to automate everything from home automation systems to office workflows.

Using the iPhone for Work

With the rise of remote work and digital collaboration, the iPhone 16 has become an essential tool for professionals. Whether you're managing emails, scanning documents, or setting up a secure VPN connection, the iPhone offers a range of productivity features that can help you stay connected and efficient.

1. Productivity Apps

Apple's built-in apps like Mail, Calendar, and Notes provide a solid foundation for productivity, but for power users, third-party apps can take your workflow to the next level.

Recommended Productivity Apps:

- **Microsoft Office Suite:** The Word, Excel, and PowerPoint apps provide all the tools you need to create, edit, and share documents from your iPhone. With cloud integration, you can access your files from OneDrive and collaborate with others in real time.

Whether you're drafting reports, analyzing data, or creating presentations, the Office Suite remains a top choice for business users.

- **Slack:** For team communication and collaboration, Slack is an essential app for remote work. With organized channels, direct messaging, and integrations with tools like Google Drive and Asana, Slack keeps your team connected and on the same page, whether you're working from the office or on the go.

- **Notion:** A highly flexible app, Notion combines note-taking, project management, and team collaboration in one platform. It allows you to create databases, wikis, task boards, and documents, making it a comprehensive tool for professionals. You can organize tasks, track progress, and collaborate with team members seamlessly from your iPhone.

2. VPN Setup and Security

In today's remote working environment, protecting your data and ensuring secure connections is crucial.

Setting up a VPN (Virtual Private Network) on your iPhone can help encrypt your internet traffic and ensure your data remains secure, especially when using public Wi-Fi networks.

How to Set Up a VPN on iPhone:

1. Go to Settings > General > VPN & Device Management.

2. Tap Add VPN Configuration.

3. Select the type of VPN (e.g., IPSec, L2TP, or IKEv2) and enter the necessary credentials provided by your VPN service.

4. Tap Done to save the configuration, then toggle on the VPN whenever you need to connect securely.

Alternatively, you can use a VPN app like NordVPN, ExpressVPN, or ProtonVPN to simplify the setup process.

Recommended VPN Apps:

- **NordVPN:** Known for its speed and robust security features, NordVPN offers easy setup, fast connections, and a no-logs policy to ensure your browsing activity remains private.

- **ExpressVPN:** Another highly rated VPN service, ExpressVPN offers strong encryption, a wide network of servers, and apps for all major platforms, making it a great choice for professionals who need secure internet access on the go.

- **ProtonVPN:** If you're looking for a free VPN option, ProtonVPN provides high levels of security without sacrificing performance, though its free tier comes with some limitations on server access and speed.

3. Document Scanning and Remote Working

With built-in document scanning and third-party apps, your iPhone 16 can replace the need for bulky scanners and paper filing systems.

Scanning Documents with iPhone:

The Notes app has a built-in document scanner that allows you to capture high-quality scans of documents, receipts, or forms.

- *Open the Notes app and create a new note.*

- *Tap the camera icon, then select Scan Documents.*

- *Position the document in the frame, and the app will automatically capture it.*

- *You can edit the scan (crop, rotate, etc.) and save it directly in your Notes or share it via email, messages, or cloud storage.*

For more advanced scanning options, apps like Genius Scan and Adobe Scan offer features such as batch scanning, automatic edge detection, and text recognition (OCR) to digitize documents quickly and accurately.

Enhancing Gaming Performance

The iPhone 16 is a powerful gaming device, capable of running high-quality games with impressive graphics and smooth performance. Whether you're a casual gamer or a serious competitor, there are several tips and tools to enhance your gaming experience.

1. Improving Performance

For optimal gaming performance, it's important to manage your device settings to ensure smooth gameplay, fast load times, and minimal interruptions.

Tips for Improving Gaming Performance:

- **Turn on Low Power Mode:** While Low Power Mode is generally used to conserve battery, enabling it during gaming sessions can reduce background activity and focus the device's resources on your game.

- **Clear Background Apps:** Before starting a game, close any unnecessary apps running in the background. This frees up

RAM and processing power, ensuring your game runs smoothly.

- Enable Do Not Disturb: Prevent distractions by enabling Do Not Disturb while playing. This silences notifications, calls, and messages, ensuring you stay focused on the game.

- Update iOS and Games: Make sure your iPhone and games are updated to the latest versions. Game updates often include performance optimizations and bug fixes that improve overall gameplay.

2. Using Game Controllers

While touchscreen controls work well for many games, some genres—such as racing, fighting, and first-person shooters—are better played with a physical controller. The iPhone 16 supports a variety of Bluetooth controllers, including popular options like Xbox and PlayStation controllers.

How to Connect a Controller to an iPhone:

1. Turn on your controller and put it into pairing mode (usually by holding down the pairing button).

2. Go to Settings > Bluetooth on your iPhone and wait for the controller to appear under Other Devices.

3. Tap the controller to pair it with your iPhone.

Once connected, you can use the controller with any compatible game, offering a more immersive and precise gaming experience.

3. Maximizing Apple Arcade

Apple Arcade offers a subscription-based gaming platform with over 200 premium games, all free from ads and in-app purchases. Whether you enjoy puzzle games, RPGs, or multiplayer experiences, Apple Arcade has something for everyone.

Tips for Maximizing Your Apple Arcade Experience:

- **Explore Genres:** With games across categories like Action, Adventure, Family, and Puzzle, Apple Arcade offers a wide variety of experiences. Explore different genres to discover new games that suit your tastes.

- **Sync Progress Across Devices:** With iCloud, your game progress is synced across all your Apple devices. This means you can start a game on your iPhone and continue it on your iPad or Mac without losing any progress.

- **Use a Game Controller:** Many Apple Arcade games are designed to work with controllers, offering a more console-like experience on your iPhone.

By leveraging the power of third-party apps, maximizing the iPhone 16's built-in productivity features, and optimizing your gaming performance, you can unlock the full potential of your device. Whether you're using task managers to organize your life, setting up a VPN for secure remote work, or enhancing your gaming experience with Apple Arcade, there are endless ways to make your iPhone 16 work harder for you. With the right tools and techniques, you can truly maximize your iPhone experience and enjoy its versatility in every aspect of your digital life.

CHAPTER 16

FAQs AND USER TIPS

*****

The iPhone 16 is packed with cutting-edge technology and a variety of features that can transform how you interact with the world. Yet, with so many features and settings, it's natural for users to have questions about how to get the most out of their devices. In this chapter, we'll answer some of the most frequently asked questions (FAQs) about the iPhone 16 and share user tips from tech experts and experienced users to help you make the most of your iPhone.

Frequently Asked Questions (FAQs)

1. How do I preserve battery life on my iPhone 16?

With all the advanced features the iPhone 16 has to offer, users often wonder how to maximize their battery life without compromising on performance.

Here are some tips:

- **Enable Low Power Mode:** This can be activated from Settings > Battery or Control Center. It reduces background processes, like automatic downloads and email fetching, to preserve the battery.

- **Manage Screen Brightness:** Reduce the brightness by going to Settings > Display & Brightness or swipe down from the top-right corner to adjust brightness manually in Control Center. Enabling Auto-Brightness also helps optimize battery life by adjusting screen brightness based on ambient light conditions.

- **Turn Off Location Services:** Constantly running GPS can drain your battery. Turn off location services for apps that don't need them by going to Settings >

Privacy > Location Services and toggling them off individually.

- Disable Background App Refresh: Background App Refresh allows apps to update content even when you're not using them, which can drain your battery. Turn it off by going to Settings > General > Background App Refresh and selecting Off or limiting it to Wi-Fi only.

2. How do I free up storage space on my iPhone 16?

Running low on storage can affect your device's performance and limit what you can store on your iPhone.

To free up space:

- Review Storage Usage: Go to Settings > General > iPhone Storage to see which apps and media are using the most space.

- Offload Unused Apps: Enable this feature to remove apps you don't use regularly without deleting their data. This option is available in Settings >

General > iPhone Storage and will automatically offload apps while keeping your documents and data intact.

- Clear Cache and Temporary Files: Certain apps, especially browsers, store cached files that can accumulate over time. In Safari, go to Settings > Safari > Clear History and Website Data to clear the cache.

- Optimize Photos: In Settings > Photos, you can turn on Optimize iPhone Storage. This keeps smaller versions of photos on your device while storing the full-resolution images in iCloud.

3. Can I use Face ID with a mask on?

Yes! With iOS 15.4 and later, Apple introduced an option to use Face ID while wearing a mask.

To set this up:

1. Go to Settings > Face ID & Passcode.

2. Toggle on Face ID with a Mask.

3. Follow the prompts to scan your face while wearing a mask.

4. What should I do if my iPhone 16 is overheating?

Overheating can occur if your iPhone is exposed to high temperatures for extended periods or if it's under heavy usage, like gaming or video streaming. Here's how to cool it down:

- **Turn Off Unnecessary Features:** Turn off background features like Bluetooth, Wi-Fi, or Location Services if they are not in use.

- **Close Power-Intensive Apps:** Double-tap the Home button or swipe up from the bottom of the screen to access the App Switcher, then swipe up on apps that you aren't using.

- **Avoid Direct Sunlight:** Keep your iPhone out of direct sunlight, especially when charging.

- **Remove the Case:** Cases can sometimes trap heat. If your phone is overheating, remove the case to allow for better ventilation.

5. How can I make the most of the camera on my iPhone 16?

The iPhone 16's camera offers impressive features like ProRAW, ProRes, and enhanced low-light capabilities.

Here's how to get the best out of your camera:

- **Use Night Mode:** The iPhone 16 automatically detects when lighting is low and will suggest using Night Mode. This feature brightens your photos without losing detail. To adjust Night Mode, tap the Night Mode icon and use the slider to increase or decrease the exposure.

- **Shoot in ProRAW:** For professionals, shooting in ProRAW offers uncompressed image data, which is ideal for detailed photo editing. Enable it in Settings > Camera > Formats, and turn on Apple ProRAW.

- **Use the Ultrawide and Telephoto Lenses:** Experiment with the Ultra Wide lens for landscape shots or group photos, and switch to the Telephoto lens for portraits or distant subjects.

6. How do I set up dual SIM on my iPhone 16?

The iPhone 16 supports dual SIM functionality, allowing you to use both a physical SIM and an eSIM.

Here's how to set it up:

1. Go to Settings > Cellular.

2. Tap Add Cellular Plan to scan the QR code provided by your carrier or enter the activation details manually.

3. Once added, choose which line to use for Data, Calls, and Messages in the Cellular Settings.

4. You can switch between lines at any time, making it convenient for users who want separate numbers for work and personal use.

7. How do I transfer data from my old iPhone to the iPhone 16?

Transferring data to your new iPhone is simple with Quick Start.

Here's how to use it:

1. Turn on both your old and new iPhones and place them near each other.

2. A Quick Start screen will appear on your old iPhone, offering to set up the new device. Tap Continue.

3. An animation will appear on your new iPhone. Hold your old iPhone over the new device to scan the animation.

4. Enter your passcode and follow the on-screen instructions to transfer your data wirelessly. You can also restore from an iCloud or Finder/iTunes backup.

User Tips from iPhone Enthusiasts and Tech Experts

The iPhone community is filled with users who have discovered clever ways to enhance the iPhone experience. Below are some of the most useful tips shared by power users and tech experts alike.

1. Use the Back Tap for Custom Shortcuts

One of the most underrated features in iOS is Back Tap, which allows you to tap the back of your iPhone to trigger specific actions.

How to Set It Up:

1. Go to Settings > Accessibility > Touch.

2. Scroll down to Back Tap.

3. Choose either Double Tap or Triple Tap and assign actions like taking a screenshot, launching the camera, or even running a shortcut.

2. Use the Files App for Cloud Storage

Many users overlook the Files app, but it's an excellent way to manage documents, photos, and videos stored across multiple cloud services like iCloud, Google Drive, and Dropbox. You can access and organize all your files in one place without needing separate apps for each service.

How to Connect Cloud Services to Files:

1. Open the Files app and tap Browse.

2. Tap the ... (three dots) in the upper-right corner and select Edit.

3. Toggle on the services you want to connect, such as Google Drive or OneDrive.

3. Swipe to Text More Efficiently

The built-in QuickPath swipe keyboard makes typing faster by letting you swipe from one letter to another without lifting your finger. It's particularly useful for texting or composing emails on the go.

To enable or use QuickPath:

- Swipe-to-Text is enabled by default. Simply drag your finger across the keyboard from letter to letter, and your iPhone will intelligently predict the word you're typing.

- For multilingual users, QuickPath automatically switches between keyboards without needing to manually change languages.

4. Protect Your Privacy with Hide My Email

For users concerned about privacy, Hide My Email in iCloud+ allows you to generate random email addresses that forward messages to your inbox. This way, you don't need to share your real email address when signing up for services.

How to Use Hide My Email:

1. Go to Settings > [Your Name] > iCloud > Hide My Email.

2. Tap Create New Address to generate a random email.

3. Use this address when signing up for newsletters, services, or websites that may send spam.

5. Use Do Not Disturb for Specific Focus Modes

Focus Modes in iOS 16 allow you to customize Do Not Disturb settings based on specific activities, like work, sleep, or personal time.

How to Set Up Focus Modes:

1. Go to Settings > Focus and choose a pre-set mode like Work or Sleep.

2. Customize which apps and contacts can send you notifications during that time.

3. You can also create custom Focus modes for specific situations, such as driving or working out, by choosing Custom and setting up your preferred settings.

6. Use FaceTime Audio for Clearer Calls

While FaceTime is commonly known for video calls, FaceTime Audio offers crystal-clear voice calls over Wi-Fi or cellular data. It's a great alternative to traditional calls, especially in areas with weak cellular reception but strong Wi-Fi.

How to Make a FaceTime Audio Call:

1. Open the FaceTime app and select a contact.

2. Tap Audio instead of Video to initiate a voice-only call.

3. You can also use Siri to say, "FaceTime Audio [Contact Name]," for a hands-free experience.

FaceTime Audio uses less data than video calls and offers much better sound quality compared to standard cellular calls.

The iPhone 16 is a versatile and powerful tool, but knowing how to troubleshoot common issues, customize settings, and utilize expert tips can significantly enhance your experience. By following the FAQs and user tips outlined in this chapter, you'll not only become more proficient with your iPhone, but you'll also unlock new ways to maximize its capabilities, making your device an essential part of your daily routine. Whether you're improving productivity, preserving battery life, or enhancing security, these strategies will ensure you get the most out of your iPhone 16.

BONUS CHAPTER

HIDDEN FEATURES

*****

The iPhone 16 is packed with powerful capabilities that most users are familiar with—calling, messaging, photography, and app usage. However, there are plenty of hidden features and fun Easter eggs that can take your experience to the next level. These little-known tools, gestures, and Siri commands can help you use your iPhone more efficiently and even add a bit of fun to your daily tasks. In this bonus chapter, we'll explore these hidden gems to ensure you're making the most of your iPhone 16.

Secret Siri Commands

Siri, Apple's voice assistant, is well-known for answering questions, setting reminders, and making calls. But beyond the basics, Siri has a range of secret commands and fun responses that can surprise and delight users. Here are some hidden Siri features and Easter eggs you can explore.

1. Roll a Dice or Flip a Coin

Sometimes you need to make quick decisions, and Siri can help you with that.

- "Hey Siri, roll a dice": Siri will roll a virtual dice and give you a random number between 1 and 6.

- "Hey Siri, flip a coin": Siri will flip a virtual coin and give you either heads or tails.

This is perfect for those moments when you need to make an unbiased decision.

2. Ask for a Joke or Fun Fact

Siri isn't just practical—she's also pretty entertaining. You can ask her for a joke, a random fact, or even some clever quips.

- *"Hey Siri, tell me a joke": Siri will provide a dad joke or a funny one-liner.*

- *"Hey Siri, give me a fun fact": Siri will share a random trivia fact that you may not know.*

- *"Hey Siri, beatbox": For a bit of fun, Siri will try her best at beatboxing.*

These little features add a fun element to Siri and can lighten up your day.

3. Siri Easter Eggs

Siri also has some hidden, playful responses to certain phrases or pop culture references. Here are a few examples:

- *"Hey Siri, I see a little silhouette of a man":* Siri may respond with lyrics from Queen's Bohemian Rhapsody.

- *"Hey Siri, what's zero divided by zero?":* This infamous response includes a reference to a Cookie Monster analogy.

- *"Hey Siri, what's the meaning of life?":* Siri offers humorous or philosophical answers to this question, often referencing the famous line from The Hitchhiker's Guide to the Galaxy.

Hidden Gestures

The iPhone 16 is full of hidden gestures that can make navigation faster and more intuitive. Here are some lesser-known gestures that can enhance your experience.

1. Tap the Back of Your iPhone for Custom Actions

Back Tap, a feature introduced in iOS 14, allows you to assign actions to double or triple taps on the back of your iPhone. This gesture can be incredibly useful for shortcuts like taking a screenshot, locking your screen, or launching an app.

How to Enable Back Tap:

1. Go to Settings > Accessibility > Touch.

2. Scroll down to Back Tap.

3. Choose Double Tap or Triple Tap and assign actions from a list of options.

You can even trigger a Shortcut through Back Tap, allowing for advanced automation with just a tap on the back of your phone.

2. Swipe with Three Fingers to Undo or Redo

If you often make mistakes while typing or editing, there's no need to shake your phone to undo the last action. Instead, you can use three-finger gestures for a more efficient approach.

- *Swipe left with three fingers to undo your last action (such as typing or editing).*

- *Swipe right with three fingers to redo an undone action.*

This simple trick is particularly useful when working with text or documents.

3. Quickly Move Between Apps

For multitasking power users, there's an easy way to switch between apps without opening the App

Switcher. You can swipe directly between apps with just a simple gesture.

- Swipe left or right along the bottom of the screen (just above the Home indicator) to move between recently used apps.

This gesture allows for a smoother transition between apps and keeps you in the flow of your work or browsing.

4. Pinch to Copy and Paste

You can copy and paste content using gestures instead of the traditional tap-and-hold method.

- Three-finger pinch inwards to copy.

- Three-finger pinch outwards to paste.

This gesture is quick and can be especially helpful when copying and pasting text or images between apps.

Hidden iPhone Tricks

In addition to gestures, there are several hidden tricks in the iPhone's settings and apps that can improve your workflow or add an extra layer of convenience to your daily use.

1. Customize Control Center

While most users know that they can access common settings from the Control Center, not everyone realizes that this panel can be fully customized with shortcuts to various tools and features.

How to Customize Control Center:

1. Go to Settings > Control Center.

2. Tap + or - to add or remove controls.

You can add shortcuts for Screen Recording, Voice Memos, Magnifier, Low Power Mode, and even Quick Note to make your frequently used features more accessible.

2. Use Spotlight for Advanced Searches

Spotlight Search is a powerful tool that can do more than just find apps or contacts. You can use it for advanced queries and actions:

- Currency Conversions: Type a currency amount, such as "100 USD to EUR," and Spotlight will instantly show the conversion.

- Perform Calculations: Type a math problem like "45 12," and Spotlight will calculate the answer.

- Find Specific Settings: Searching for a particular setting, like "Bluetooth," will bring up the relevant toggle directly in the search results.

Spotlight Search is often overlooked but can save time when performing quick calculations or looking for hidden settings.

3. Customize Safari's Start Page

With iOS 16, Safari's start page is more customizable than ever. You can add favorite websites, customize the background, and even show your reading list or iCloud tabs.

How to Customize Safari's Start Page:

1. Open Safari and scroll to the bottom of the start page.

2. Tap Edit.

3. Toggle features like Favorites, Reading List, and Siri Suggestions on or off. You can also choose a background image to personalize your start page.

This makes Safari feel more tailored to your needs, allowing you to access your favorite sites and resources faster.

4. Measure Height with the Measure App

The Measure app on your iPhone can do more than just calculate distances. It can also measure a person's height using Augmented Reality (AR) technology.

How to Measure Someone's Height:

1. Open the Measure app.

2. Point the camera at the person you want to measure, making sure their entire body fits in the frame.

3. After a moment, the app will display their height at the top of the screen.

This tool is great for quick measurements without the need for a ruler or tape measure.

5. Add Custom Text Replacements

If you often type out long words or phrases, Text Replacement can save you time by turning shortcodes into full sentences.

How to Set Up Text Replacement:

1. Go to Settings > General > Keyboard > Text Replacement.

2. Tap the + icon to create a new shortcut.

3. Enter the phrase you want to use (e.g., "On my way") and the shortcut (e.g., "omw").

Now, whenever you type "omw," your iPhone will automatically replace it with "On my way."

Fun Easter Eggs in iPhone Apps

There are several fun and quirky Easter eggs hidden in various apps that add an extra layer of enjoyment to using your iPhone.

1. Send Special Effects in iMessage

iMessage has a hidden feature that lets you send messages with special effects. You can make messages more exciting by adding animations like fireworks, confetti, or a laser show.

How to Use Special Effects in iMessage:

1. Type your message in iMessage, but before sending, press and hold the Send button (the upward arrow).

2. This will bring up the Send with Effect menu, where you can choose from Bubble effects (like Slam or Gentle) or Screen effects (like Balloons or Fireworks).

This feature can be a fun way to add some flair to your conversations.

2. Change the Flashlight Intensity

Many people use the flashlight feature on their iPhones, but few know that you can adjust its brightness to different levels.

How to Change Flashlight Intensity:

1. Swipe down from the top-right corner to open Control Center.

2. Tap and hold the Flashlight icon.

3. A slider will appear, allowing you to adjust the brightness from dim to full strength.

This is useful for times when you need a softer light or want to conserve battery.

3. See When Messages Were Sent

In the Messages app, you can view the exact time any message was sent or received by using a simple hidden gesture.

How to View Message Timestamps:

1. Open any conversation in the

Messages app

2. Swipe left on the screen, and the timestamps for all messages will appear on the right side.

This can be particularly handy for tracking the timing of conversations.

The iPhone 16 is a device filled with countless hidden features and fun Easter eggs that can make everyday tasks more enjoyable and efficient. Whether you're using secret Siri commands for entertainment, taking advantage of hidden gestures for faster navigation, or discovering new tricks in iPhone apps, these lesser-known capabilities can help you unlock the full potential of your device. By exploring these hidden gems, you'll gain a deeper understanding of how versatile and fun the iPhone 16 can be.

GLOSSARY OF TERMS

A

- **AirDrop:** A feature that allows iPhone users to share files, photos, and other data wirelessly with nearby Apple devices.

- **App Library:** A feature that automatically organizes all your apps into categories, located at the end of the Home Screen pages.

- **Apple Pay:** A mobile payment and digital wallet service that lets users make payments using their iPhone, Apple Watch, or other Apple devices.

- **AssistiveTouch:** An accessibility feature that provides an on-screen menu to perform gestures and actions without pressing physical buttons.

B

- **Back Tap:** A feature that allows users to trigger specific actions by tapping the back of the iPhone.

- **Background App Refresh:** A setting that allows apps to refresh their content in the background when connected to Wi-Fi or cellular data.

C

- **Control Center:** A panel that gives quick access to essential settings like Wi-Fi, Bluetooth, Airplane Mode, and brightness adjustments.

- **Cinematic Mode:** A video feature that automatically adjusts the depth of field and focuses on subjects, similar to portrait mode for photos.

D

- **Do Not Disturb:** A feature that silences calls, alerts, and notifications when activated. It can be customized to allow certain contacts or apps to break through.

E

- **eSIM:** A digital SIM card embedded in the iPhone that allows users to activate cellular service without needing a physical SIM card.

- **Exposure:** A photography setting that controls the amount of light allowed into the camera sensor, affecting the brightness of the image.

F

- **Face ID:** Apple's facial recognition technology is used to unlock the iPhone and authenticate payments.

- **Focus Mode:** A customizable feature that limits distractions by filtering notifications and apps based on specific activities like work or sleep.

G

- **Gesture:** Touch-based commands like swiping, pinching, or tapping to control the iPhone's interface or perform actions.

H

- **Handoff:** A feature that allows users to start a task on one Apple device and continue it on another, such as transferring a phone call from the iPhone to a Mac.

- **HDR:** High Dynamic Range, a photography feature that captures more detail in both the bright and dark areas of an image.

I

- **iCloud:** Apple's cloud storage service that syncs data like photos, files, and backups across devices.

- **iCloud Backup:** An automatic backup feature that saves your iPhone's data to iCloud so it can be restored later if needed.

- **iMessage:** Apple's proprietary messaging service that allows users to send texts, photos, and videos over Wi-Fi or cellular data to other Apple devices.

L

- **Live Listen:** A feature that lets users turn their iPhone into a remote microphone to help improve hearing in noisy environments when using AirPods or hearing aids.

M

- **Magnifier:** An accessibility feature that turns the iPhone's camera into a magnifying glass for enlarging text and objects.

- **Memoji:** Personalized animated emojis that mimic the user's facial expressions and can be used in iMessages and FaceTime.

N

- **Night Mode:** A camera feature that enhances low-light photos by brightening them without reducing detail.

P

- **Picture-in-Picture (PiP):** A multitasking feature that allows users to watch videos or make FaceTime calls in a small window while using other apps.

- **Private Relay:** A privacy feature in iCloud+ that encrypts and hides your browsing activity by routing your internet traffic through multiple servers.

Q

- **Quick Start:** A feature that simplifies the process of transferring data from an old iPhone to a new one using proximity and wireless technology.

R

- **Reachability:** A feature that lowers the top half of the iPhone screen, making it easier to access for one-handed use.

S

- **Shortcuts:** An automation app that lets users create custom workflows and tasks to be executed with a single tap or voice command.

- **Spatial Audio:** A feature that creates an immersive 3D audio experience by tracking the user's head movements with the sound source.

T

- **True Tone:** A display feature that adjusts the color balance of the screen to match the ambient lighting, making content easier on the eyes.

- **Touch ID:** A fingerprint recognition feature used to unlock the iPhone and authenticate payments (available on select models).

U

- **Ultra Wide Lens:** A camera lens that captures more of the scene by offering a wider field of view.

V

- VoiceOver: An accessibility feature that reads aloud text and screen content, helping visually impaired users navigate the iPhone.

W

- Widgets: Customizable app previews that display real-time information (like weather or calendar events) directly on the Home Screen.

Printed in Dunstable, United Kingdom